ANTON CHEKHOV AT THE MOSCOW ART THEATRE

The Moscow Art Theatre is still recognised as having more impact on modern theatre than any company in the world. This lavishly illustrated book is a beautifully crafted reproduction of a Russian journal from 1914 and documents, photographically, the premieres of Anton Chekhov's full-length plays produced by the Moscow Art Theatre, including:

- *Seagull*
- *Three Sisters*
- *Uncle Vanya*
- *Cherry Orchard*, and
- *Ivanov*.

Edited by renowned theatre historian Vera Gottlieb, the volume also reproduces – for the first time in an English translation – introductions by Stanislavsky's collaborator Nemirovich-Danchenko and a fascinating introduction by Nikolai Efros, the first literary manager of the MAT, and the first author of monographs on Chekhov's plays at the MAT. With 198 illustrations, many of which are unfamiliar, this is a significant contribution to our own understanding of the origins of today's theatre.

Vera Gottlieb is Research Professor in Drama at Goldsmiths College, University of London, and Director of the Pinter Centre for Research in Performance. She has previously translated *A Chekhov Quartet* (1996) and is the co-editor of *The Cambridge Companion to Chekhov* (2000).

ANTON CHEKHOV AT THE MOSCOW ART THEATRE

Archive Illustrations of the Original Productions

Translated and edited by
Vera Gottlieb

From the original journal edited by Nikolai Efros, 1914

Routledge
Taylor & Francis Group

LONDON AND NEW YORK

First published 2005 by Routledge
2 Park Square, Milton Park, Abingdon, Oxon OX14 4RN

Simultaneously published in the USA and Canada
by Routledge
270 Madison Ave, New York, NY 10016

Routledge is an imprint of the Taylor & Francis Group

Typeset in Janson Text by Keystroke, Jacaranda Lodge, Wolverhampton
Printed and bound in Great Britain by
TJ International Ltd, Padstow, Cornwall

British Library Cataloguing in Publication Data
A catalogue record for this book is available from the British Library

Library of Congress Cataloging in Publication Data
Anton Chekhov at the Moscow Art Theatre : archive illustrations
of the original productions / [edited by] Vera Gottlieb.
    p. cm.
    'This lavishly illustrated book is a beautifully crafted reproduction of
a Russian journal [i.e. photographs collected by Nikolai Efros] from
1914 and documents, photographically, the premieres of all of Anton
Chekhov's plays produced by the Moscow Art Theatre. . . also
reproduces – for the first time in an English translation – introductions
by Stanislavsky's collaborators Nemirovich-Danchenko and Efros'
Includes bibliographical references.
    1. Chekhov, Anton Pavlovich, 1860–1904—Stage history—Pictorial
works. 2. Chekhov, Anton Pavlovich, 1860–1904—Dramatic
production—Pictorial works. 3. Moskovskii khudozhestvennyi
akademicheskii teatr—Pictorial works. I. Gottlieb, Vera, 1945–
II. Efros, N. E. (Nikolai Efimovich), 1867–1923. III. Moskovskii
khudozhestvennyi akademicheskii teatr.
    PG3458.Z9S823 2004
    891.72'3—dc22   2004015535

ISBN 0–415–34440–9

CONTENTS

LIST OF ILLUSTRATIONS

INTRODUCTION

Vera Gottlieb

Some years ago I was working at home when a family friend rang – it was Liliana Archibald, whose parents Dr Noah and Sophie Barou, had been friends of my parents. They had left Russia after the Revolution and as highly cultured collectors, they had some marvellous pictures and books. Liliana was ringing to tell me that she was clearing their basement, and to ask if I was interested in looking at anything. If I was, I needed to come quickly before the bonfire devoured papers and whatever else seemingly served no purpose.

It was in their basement that I found this extraordinary collection by Nikolai Efros of the illustrations of the Moscow Art Theatre's premieres of all of Chekhov's five major plays, and I am deeply grateful to Liliana for giving me the opportunity to rescue it.

Initially it was to be published by Gordon and Breach's Harwood Academic Press under their Russian Theatre Archive, edited by John Freedman and Anatoly Smeliansky in Moscow, and Leon Gitelman in St Petersburg working with Robert Robertson in London. Time went by and I was side-tracked by other work, but then Harwood took the original and with great care sent it to a specialist photographer in Southampton. The original was – and is – very fragile, and appears more like a hand-made scrapbook. Published in St Petersburg in 1914, it has been printed on different colours and types of paper; it is a mixture of studio photographs and seemingly of specific moments on stage from each of the five full-length plays. There are four superb colour designs by Viktor Simov, the Moscow Art Theatre scenographer; and studio photographs of Chekhov, and of different actors, as well as of Stanislavski and Nemirovich-Danchenko, the famous co-founders of the Moscow Art Theatre in 1898. In total, it is more like a Brecht model book than anything I had previously seen of visual material on Chekhov's productions, even when I was lucky enough to handle archive material such as Stanislavski's original prompt copy of the first MAT *Seagull* in the old Moscow Art Theatre.

That is not, of course, to claim absolute originality for individual illustrations – many are published elsewhere, either in books on Chekhov or in books on Russian theatre or on scenography, but some *are* unfamiliar, while it is the collection as a whole which seems unusual. I had not previously seen such a mass of visual material from the premiere productions. It must be said, however, that only after 1902 were photographs actually taken in the theatre – until then, they are much more likely to be studio photographs, set up to look like production photos. And although Efros does not say so explicitly, the photographs of the production of *Seagull* must be from the 1905 revival, *not* the premiere in 1898, given the theatrical nature of the photographs. While that accounts for the variation, not all the photographers of those productions have been credited, while the photographs of Chekhov, the actors and other moments – such as the first read-through of *Seagull* – *were* taken by credited photographers: Sredin, Vasilevski, Gusev, and the majority of production photos by Scherer and Nabholtz, and Fisher.

With a research grant from the Drama Department of Goldsmiths College, University of London, I set out to find other copies of the collection and, indeed, whether it had ever been translated and re-published. As far as I can establish, there is no record of such a collection in the Bibliothèque Nationale in Paris; in the British Library in London; or in the Library of Congress. It may, of course, have been filed in a way which made it difficult to track; equally, I do know that there must be others in private hands. But it has not been published again in its original 1914 form, edited by Nikolai Efros, with a brief introduction by Nemirovich-Danchenko, and a longer one by Efros himself. Again, I must stress that many images are familiar from other sources – such as *Le Théâtre Artistique de Moscou (1898–1917)*, by Claudine Amiard-Chevrel, in the excellent Editions du Centre National de la Recherche Scientifique, Paris 1979. This is one in the series *Collection 'Le Chœur des Muses'*. In his thorough and very useful *The Chekhov Theatre*, (Cambridge: CUP, 1997), Laurence Senelick has reproduced some of the illustrations. but there is no mention of this collection in either of those major sources – or, indeed, in any other publication which I have seen in English, French or Russian. In the long list of publications by Efros in various histories and encyclopaedia entries, there is just one entry almost identical to that of this collection, but dated 1919: *Plays of A.P. Chekhov in MAT productions*, Petersburg, and it is probable that it is indeed this collection, either inaccurately dated or – less likely – perhaps reprinted.

In the majority of books on Chekhov – in, for instance, Ronald Hingley's authoritative *A Life of Chekhov* (London: Oxford University Press, 1976), or other critical, biographical, or historical works on Chekhov – Efros, the first Literary Manager of the Moscow Art Theatre, is either not mentioned or given a passing reference, and that in not always very complimentary terms given Chekhov's seeming dislike of Efros.

This publication was delayed by a number of factors: first Gordon and Breach was taken over by Routledge as part of Taylor & Francis's take-over of Routledge itself. And during that time of muddle and change, the specialist photographs – so carefully done in Southampton – were simply lost. A long search failed to produce them, and this has meant that the photographs have had to be redone – making the original even more fragile! But the process of scanning is in itself fascinating. and has improved since Harwood first had the illustrations rather expensively photographed.

The 'scrapbook' feel of the original is something I had initially hoped to reproduce. but costs have inevitably stopped the publication from being a 'facsimile', and it seems more important to ensure that it is as accessible as possible rather than sacrificing access.bility to reproducing the four full-colour Simov designs (which *are* reproduced in other publications), or the use of different colour paper, or the use of basic glue to stick on some loose illustrations! It is the entity which matters – and, indeed, the extraordinary prescience Efros showed in 1914 in writing about the plays as he does. While his introduction may seem repetitive and effusive, first it must be remembered that he is using a critical tone of the time, adopted by some theatre historians and critics; and second, it is ultimately more significant that he recognized the originality and innovatory nature of the plays at a time when almost nobody had written about them as a whole or in depth. In this sense, as Anatoly Smeliansky rightly reminded me, Efros did critically what Stanislavski and Nemirovich-Danchenko did practically: all three – in spite of the conflicts between them *and* with Chekhov – first brought the plays to an audience, whether in production or as play texts.

One need only read the descriptions of the ill-fated first

production in 1896 of *Seagull* at Petersburg's Aleksandrinski Theatre, to realize quite how strange these plays were to Chekhov's contemporaries: seemingly plotless, with inconclusive endings, and either a breach of dramatic convention *or* – more significantly – Chekhov's still sometimes misunderstood inversion and thus deliberate subversion of theatre conventions. It is more equivalent to the first reactions to Beckett's *Waiting for Godot* – a play misunderstood not only by some of its first audiences, but also by many critics, and other practitioners. Chekhov did not suffer from the same constant critical abuse as did Ibsen with most of his plays, in particular *Ghosts, A Doll's House* or *Hedda Gabler*, but he never really regained confidence after the disastrous premiere of *Seagull* in spite of the comparative success of most of the MAT productions of his plays. And most of the conflicts Chekhov had with Stanislavski were over the interpretation of the plays, over the issues of 'tone' and whether Chekhov should be taken seriously when he subtitled *Seagull* and *Cherry Orchard* 'comedies', and resolutely avoided any sense of tragedy in the subtitling of the other major plays: *Uncle Vanya* is 'scenes from country life'; *Three Sisters* is subtitled 'a drama' – namely, a play of serious intent; while *Ivanov* is simply 'a play in four acts'.

Efros also suggests the serious conflicts over casting, over the famous rows about sound effects (see Endnote 37), and to a certain extent takes at face value Chekhov's wry or ironic comments, thus in tandem with Stanislavski implanting the idea – so often contradicted in the letters – that Chekhov was too shy and retiring to get really angry about the productions of his plays. The idea of the mutual love affair between Chekhov and the MAT is very much present in this publication – as it is in Stanislavski's *My Life in Art*. Stanislavski was also, however, remarkably honest about his first reaction to *Seagull* (which he disliked) and then about the mistakes he subsequently made. And it is crucial to remember that most non-Russian speakers and readers have the misleading and often distorted Elizabeth Hapgood versions of Stanislavski's works. Only with Laurence Senelick's *The Chekhov Theatre* or Jean Benedetti's *The Moscow Art Theatre Letters* and his biography, *Stanislavski*, have some of the most serious misreadings been corrected. Hopefully Anatoly Smeliansky's forthcoming book on Stanislavski will provide the final nail in the coffin of the distorted American translations.

As Literary Manager, however, Efros was in a particularly difficult position. Often caught between dramatist and director, and sometimes also the cast, the role of literary manager or dramaturg is historically fraught with ambiguity, conflicts of interest and requests for advice which are often ignored.

Nikolai Efimovich Efros was born in 1867 and died on 6 June 1923. A graduate of the Law Faculty of Moscow University, in 1891 he started writing theatre reviews. Initially a prominent journalist, he became the leading theatre critic of the newspaper *Russkie vedomosti* (*The Russian Gazette*), and also wrote reviews of Moscow theatre productions for the newspapers *Teatral* (*Playgoer*) and, among others, for *Novosti dnia* (*News of the Day*) and the Moscow *Kur'er* (*Courier*). With the opening of the Moscow Art Theatre by Stanislavski and Nemirovich-Danchenko in 1898, Efros became the MAT's first Literary Manager, supporting both their productions and their school of acting. He spoke German and French, and in 1899 translated Hauptmann's *Lonely Lives* (or *The Lonely Ones – Einsame Menschen*, 1890. See Endnote 44) for the MAT, and Victor Hugo's *Angels*. In 1910 he wrote his own play, but his main gift lay in theatre criticism and theatre history. Efros authored numerous monographs on such great Russian actors as Mikhail Shchepkin, Alexander Yuzhin (Sumbatov), actor and dramatist of the Maly Theatre, the great Maria Nikolaevna Ermolova (or Yermolova), leading actress at the Maly Theatre, and on Kachalov and others. In 1919 Efros wrote detailed monographs on *Three Sisters* and *Cherry Orchard*. Efros was the author of the first book on Stanislavski in 1918, and in 1914 – the same year as this collection of Chekhov's plays at the MAT – he edited the first volume of *Istoriia russkogo teatr* (*History of the Russian Theatre*) with V.V. Kalash.

Efros also wrote a book entitled *The Moscow Art Theatre, 1898–1923*, which has never been translated, and seemingly only previously used in Western European theatre history of Chekhov and the MAT by Claudine Amiard-Chevrel in the previously mentioned *Le Théâtre Artistique de Moscou (1898–1917)*. In *The Moscow Art Theatre, 1898–1923* (to give it an English title), Efros resolutely denies that the MAT served any ideological interests, particularly those of the educated bourgeoisie, but as Senelick has pointed out: 'Though the white-collar class discovered its own malaise reflected so authentically, Chekhov and the Art Theatre still remained caviare to the general' (*The Chekhov Theatre*, p.55).

The contribution Efros made to his contemporary theatre, to serious analysis of Chekhov's plays in production, and to the role, function and workings of the Moscow Art Theatre have too long been neglected. One may disagree with his interpretations, but it is invaluable and fascinating to have such a mine of contemporary material, whether visual or verbal.

After the Bolshevik Revolution of 1917, Efros wrote for the new theatre journals, such as *Kultura teatra* (*Theatre Culture*), and then worked in the historical-theatrical section of the newly formed TEO – the Theatrical Department of the People's Commissariat of Education. Anatoly Lunacharsky, the highly enlightened People's Commissar (Narkom) for Education (which, of course, included the arts), appointed Meyerhold the Head of the TEO in 1920. There may be some irony in Efros working under Meyerhold given his less than complimentary and idiosyncratic critical reaction to Meyerhold's performance as Konstantin in the MAT's first *Seagull* (albeit hard to translate given some ambiguity in tone. See Endnote 44). But it is also significant that Efros was made Chairman of the Russian Academy of Cultural Studies.

This collection, and Efros' subsequent books on the plays, their productions, and MAT actors and Stanislavski himself, make one factor abundantly clear, however, and that is Efros' love of Chekhov's plays and of the company. This was not generally reciprocated, and there were two unfortunate incidents involving Efros which incurred Chekhov's fury – one an honest mistake on Efros' part. The first row arose over the announced title of *Three Sisters*. As part of the publicity campaign, Efros had written an article which suggested that the title *Three Sisters* was a provisional one. When it was picked up by the provincial press, Chekhov reacted in an uncharacteristically furious manner – as he wrote in a letter to his wife Olga Knipper on 8 September 1900: 'Where does the news come from in *Novosti dnia* that the title *Three Sisters* is unsuitable? What utter rubbish! It may not be suitable, but I have absolutely no intention of changing it . . .'

Olga Knipper clearly had the same view of Efros, at least according to her reference to Efros while writing about the success of Nemirovich-Danchenko's new play, *In Dreams*. In a letter to Chekhov of 22 December 1901 she wrote: 'Of course, Efros either said nothing or tore people to shreds . . .'

The worst row, however, came about as a result of a sincere misunderstanding. It concerned *Cherry Orchard*, Nemirovich-Danchenko's mistake and problems of semantics, but it led to Chekhov refusing to have anything more to do with Efros (see Chekhov's letter of 23 October 1903 to Nemirovich). Essentially, Nemirovich had given Efros a description of the plot of *Cherry Orchard*, which Efros then published in *Novosti dnia*, and this article was then picked up by the *Krimski Kur'er* (*Crimean Courier*) and *Odesskie novosti* (*Odessa News*). To his horror, Chekhov read that the play was set in a hotel, and in spite of a telegram sent to *Yuzhnyi Krai* (*Southern Region*) which stated that the essay in *Novosti dnia* was 'a crude hoax which bore no relation to reality' (letter from Nemirovich to Chekhov, 30 October 1903), Chekhov was still furious. Efros was seriously embarrassed by the telegram and by Nemirovich's subsequent refusal to deny that it was a hoax, given that there *were* inaccuracies in Efros' description of the plot. The actual cause of the row, as so often in the intense and heightened atmosphere created by a new play in production, was actually a minor misunderstanding blown up given the press coverage – and Chekhov's illness. The mention of billiards in the play led Nemirovich – and Efros – to assume that it was set in a hotel, and the words for 'drawing-room' – *gostinaia* – and 'hotel' – *gostinitsa* – are very similar. Yet the row went on for some time and it was only on 5 November that Chekhov finally understood the cause, while nonetheless complaining of Efros' 'insolence' (letter to Stanislavski on the same day). Two days later, Chekhov wrote to Knipper that 'Until now all I have been worried about is that Simov will draw a hotel in Act III. That mistake must be corrected. A whole month has passed since I wrote about it, and the only response is a shrug of the shoulders. Obviously they [Nemirovich and Stanislavski] like the hotel . . .' There were also the usual tensions over casting – and, more than ever, over the interpretation of *Cherry Orchard*.

Anyone who has worked in a theatre company knows how easily rows may develop, and one of the main sources of tension was the relationship between Stanislavski and his co-founder and partner, Nemirovich-Danchenko. This has been largely glossed over in the histories of the MAT – and perhaps rightly so in that the MAT's reputation did not arise from the rows and scandals, but from the quality of the work. But it does mean that Efros' idealised view of the MAT in his introduction to this collection must be viewed through spectacles a little less rosy.

For an accurate – if wickedly mischievous – view of the MAT (significantly some 25 to 30 years later), playwright and novelist Mikhail Bulgakov's novel *Black Snow* (1936–37) is more revealing (and entertaining!) than Efros' view. The novel is a brilliant thinly veiled parody of Bulgakov's first encounter with the MAT, and the problems he had, particularly with Stanislavski, during the four years of rehearsals of Bulgakov's *Molière*. After well over three years of rehearsal Stanislavski wanted to start again from scratch as the actors had – inevitably – become bored with the lack of tangible results. Only a directorial coup by Nemirovich in late May 1935 finally got the production on – and added to Bulgakov's experiences of the MAT which had started in 1925 with his dramatised novel *The White Guard*, performed as *The Days of the Turbins*.

Professional in every way, both Stanislavski and Nemirovich kept their disagreements as private as possible, and it must be borne in mind that their collaboration, however fraught, lasted until Stanislavski's death in 1938. This was at a time under Stalin in which Stanislavski, seriously ill, risked dire political and personal consequences when he helped Meyerhold, by then already in serious trouble.

The collaboration between the two founders went back 40 years, before 1898 when they opened the MAT, and then withstood not only Stanislavski's resignation as a shareholder, but also the lesser-known fact that he resigned from the Board of Directors in 1908, and subsequently played no managerial role.

Each brought different strengths to the MAT: Nemirovich was a more subtle interpreter of plays, while Stanislavski was, as we know, not just a great actor but a great teacher, and often generous in helping his former students, whether Meyerhold or Vakhtangov, among others. Together with Nemirovich-Danchenko, Stanislavski's help also took the form of encouraging Meyerhold and Vakhtangov, in particular, to open various Studios affiliated to the MAT, and which enabled often brilliant innovatory productions and plays to find a 'home'. In his invaluable *The Moscow Art Theatre Letters*, Jean Benedetti gives a selection of letters providing a rounded picture of the relationships and feelings. It is also often the case with theatre companies that if the tensions and disagreements do not become totally destructive, sometimes the result is greater creativity and innovation. This, however, is going well beyond the time-frame of Chekhov's premieres at the MAT, and Efros' role in creating this collection.

This collection of illustrations has a clear structure to it. First, Efros provides individual photographs of Chekhov, Stanislavski, Nemirovich-Danchenko, major actors such as Kachalov, Artem and

Leonidov, and of group portraits of the MAT in Yalta, or at a restaurant in Yalta, and the – well-known – photograph of the first read-through of *Seagull* with the less familiar reaction to it. He also provides illustrations of some of the first programmes; there are four of Simov's colour designs, albeit without *Cherry Orchard*, and of Simov's models plus group portraits of the leading actors and actresses of the company. The collection then moves on to provide a play-by-play visual account. Efros gives the cast list and date of the premiere, then provides act-by-act visual demonstrations of each of the plays, often with quotations, and then marvellously detailed 'character portraits' of all the individual actors in costume and 'in character'.

On several occasions the quotations 'as captions' from the plays are either so foreshortened as to be difficult to find in the original or simply inaccurate. I have exercised an editorial privilege in correcting these, and providing the original quotation. The emphasis throughout has been to ensure that the reader may find the exact moment of action illustrated from the play and, albeit difficult, irrespective of the translation or edition or version. In addition, I have tried to clarify the character addressed in the quotation by adding the information in square brackets in the list of illustrations.

There are few collections that provide such a clear sense of the 'ensemble' which gave the MAT its unique character. It is not just the recurrence of Stanislavski's name as Trigorin in *Seagull*, as Astrov in *Uncle Vanya*, Vershinin in *Three Sisters*, Gayev in *Cherry Orchard* and Shabelski in *Ivanov*, or Knipper as Arkadina in *Seagull*, as Elena in *Uncle Vanya*, Masha in *Three Sisters*, or Ranevskaya in *Cherry Orchard*. A few actors came and went – Meyerhold left after *Seagull* in order to direct his own Studio and work elsewhere with Stanislavski's blessing, returning for *Three Sisters* to play Tuzenbakh which Kachalov then took over, a point which Efros oddly omits. And then Meyerhold played Konstantin again when he returned briefly for the revival in 1905, sharing the role with V.V. Maximov. But most remained throughout all of the premieres – and for some time afterwards. The great Artem played Shamrayev, Luzhski played Sorin; Vishnevski played Dorn, and Lilina played Masha in *Seagull*. In *Uncle Vanya*, Artem played Telegin (Waffles), Luzhski played Serebriakov, Vishnevski had the role of Uncle Vanya, while Lilina played Sonia. In *Three Sisters*, Artem played Chebutykin, Luzhski was Andrei, Vishnevski played Kulygin, and Lilina was Natasha. With *Cherry Orchard* some of the older actors gave way to younger ones, or played elsewhere, and some came back later – such as Luzhski to play Lebedev in *Ivanov*. The great Kachalov, Leonidov, Massalitinov, Gribunin, Muratova, Samarova or Moskvin, to name perhaps the greatest, all created an ensemble in which parts were exchanged for different performances or renewed – given the length of time all of the plays were in the repertoire, with the exception of *Seagull*.

From its opening in 1898, *Seagull* then left the repertory after 1905, with only 63 performances, and there was no attempt to revive it until 1916 – a revival which was postponed, and then again attempted unsuccessfully in 1919. Given a purely conventional production in 1960, described below, the play had to wait until Oleg Yefremov reinterpreted it in 1980. But it was the continuity of the *ensemble* which enabled Chekhov to request that a particular actor play a specific role – albeit a request often ignored. It was this continuity which enabled Stanislavski to develop his 'System', and the same sense of ensemble, of real company-playing, which gave the MAT its unique and innovatory nature.

All that is missing from Efros' collection are Simov's groundplans, a major visual element which may be found in Claudine Amiard-Chevrel's book, and – among others – in Alfred Bassekhes' fascinating *Khudozhniki na stsene MKhAT (Artists on the stage of the MAT)*, Moscow, 1960.

On a purely personal note, it was Alfred Bassekhes, my mother's cousin, who took me on a private backstage tour of the old MAT. He had worked with Stanislavski and the MAT as an artist and art historian, and after years in Siberia, had been 'rehabilitated'. Unfortunately I was still only about 14 at the time and although over-awed and impressed, I was too ignorant to understand who had previously stood in the wings, performed on that stage and created extraordinary performances. Nonetheless, the memory has stayed with me.

A further source of visual material is the booklet published by Iskusstvo in Moscow in 1960 by M.G. Markarov and T.S. Modestov, *P'esy A.P. Chekhova v Moskovskom Khudozhestvennom teatre*, a collection that starts with the 1898 *Seagull* and ends in 1960 with Stanitsin's MAT *Seagull*, with Tarasova playing Arkadina. This, however, was 'museum'-Chekhov, and part of the events for his 1960 jubilee year. The acting was, as always, marvellous, but as Viktor Stanitsin ominously put it: 'There is no need for a re-staging of the Chekhov plays. The present production is still in an unbroken tradition of original business and interpretations' (quoted by Senelick, *The Chekhov Theatre*, p.202).

It was to be Georgi Tovstonogov's radical reinterpretation of *Three Sisters* at the Leningrad BDT (Bolshoi Dramatic Theatre) in 1965 (towards the end of Krushchev's 'thaw') that finally started the changes in interpretation. This was then followed in 1966 by (no relation to Nikolai Efros) Anatoli Efros' controversial *Seagull* at Moscow's Lenin-Komsomol Theatre and *Three Sisters* (1967) at the Malaia Bronnaia, then – some years later – by his even more controversial *Cherry Orchard* (1975) at Moscow's famous experimental Taganka Theatre.

But the real innovation in Chekhov's own 'house' came with the productions of Oleg Yefremov – starting with *Ivanov* (1975) with Innokenti Smoktunovski (famous in the West for his role as Hamlet in Kozintsev's great film) in the title role.

It is also not accidental that *Ivanov* received ten separate productions between 1970 and 1978 – the play which had been perceived as unplayable for 80 years suddenly offered greater possibilities of experiment and innovation than the most frequently performed of Chekhov's plays. For the non-Russian-speaking reader who wishes to trace the MAT and Chekhov production both at the MAT, and elsewhere, up to 1995, Laurence Senelick's book is highly recommended. On specific Chekhov plays, and aspects of the plays in theatre and on film, see *The Cambridge Companion to Chekhov* (recommended in the Endnotes, as are other works).

Just as with the original MAT premiere productions from 1898, which first interpreted Chekhov's plays seriously, it was the MAT under Yefremov in 1975 that consolidated the complex process of *re*-interpretation. There had been other stylistic innovations such as Tairov's 1944/45 *Seagull* at Moscow's Kamerni Theatre (see my *Chekhov in Performance in Russia and Soviet Russia*), but as with the original productions in this collection, it was not until Chekhov's 'house' rediscovered his plays for new audiences, that what had become an ossified tradition was finally transformed and reinvented under Yefremov.

The ossification of MAT Chekhov was partly caused by the fact that they were considered the only true interpreters of Chekhov, but it was also in large part due to the complex and delicate relationship between Stanislavski and Stalin. Before the Revolution both Stanislavski and Nemirovich-Danchenko had been wealthy landowners, and the former also a factory owner – so it is ironic that Stanislavski came to be far more highly regarded by Stalin than the Bolshevik and Communist Meyerhold who perished at Stalin's hands. That potentially dangerous (but also awkward) approval of Stalin for Stanislavski, and Stalin's sense that the MAT's 'naturalism' somehow accorded with Socialist Realism, is a story that still remains to be told. Clearly the MAT's repertoire in the 1930s and 1940s helped to maintain the precarious balance between the two styles since the main company performed not only Chekhov and Gorki but also new Soviet plays. No doubt in his forthcoming biography of Stanislavski, Anatoly Smeliansky will throw light on this complex story.

One significant point still needs to be made about this collection and about Efros' story of Chekhov and the newly formed MAT. Like many other critics of his day, Efros says relatively little about Viktor Simov's designs of the plays. While he records the problems of individual acting performances or the conflicts over sound effects, he offers little analysis of the scenography. It is not my function here to offer an analysis that Efros omits. The idea of a unifying design concept was still as new as that of directorial vision and overall interpretation, but it is in the analysis of Stanislavski's and Nemirovich-Danchenko's innovatory roles as directors that Efros offers something unique for his time. In terms of theatre history, it was almost too early to expect a critique of the design, whether of setting or lighting. Simov's work on the plays, however, firmly established the tradition of (the then still relatively new) naturalism in the detailing, in the movement from interior to exterior, and vice versa, and in the attempt to create a lived-in individual 'home' rather than a general 'house'. This was done, of course, with the then-current mix of three-dimensional and two-dimensional elements. Thus in the setting for Act I of *Uncle Vanya* one can clearly see the painted backcloth (with floor batten), and yet three-dimensional furniture and properties. For a detailed analysis of Simov's designs of the first MAT productions, readers are recommended to use Arnold Aronson's work, in particular 'The Scenography of Chekhov' in *The Cambridge Companion to Chekhov*. Laurence Senelick's work also provides detail on the visual elements of the productions.

The issue of transliteration must be explained here. In order to ensure that the reader will be able to find the moment of action illustrated from the play, my emphasis has been to enable recognition of the names, so often differently transliterated in English. For this reason, there is not ultimately any attempt at consistency in the use of transliteration. Consistent transliteration – the usual aim of any true linguist – would have rendered some characters' names unrecognisable. Thus Yasha in *Cherry Orchard* should be transliterated as 'Iasha'; and in the same play, Gayev as 'Gaev', or Yepikhodov as 'Epikhodov', or Anya as 'Ania' and Valya as 'Valia'. I have instead used the most common English rendering of characters' names which the reader will find in Ronald Hingley's three-volume *Oxford Chekhov* or Michael Frayn's versions in Penguin's *Chekhov Plays* and other available popular collections. Given that some collections provide more exact translations (such as Hingley's), while others are very much versions (such as Frayn's or Trevor Griffiths' *Cherry Orchard*), the priority has been more immediate recognition. Where the transliteration has been more consistent with the usual convention is in the names of the actors, directors and photographers – namely, real people rather than well-known characters in the plays. Here too, however, I have used the more recognizable form where a director – such as Yefremov – is familiar in the English-speaking theatrical and critical world.

The same emphasis on accessibility has informed the translation of the quotations and, indeed, the translation as a whole. There are times when Efros' meaning is obscure or deliberately veiled. In such cases I have made educated guesses.

All dates used by Efros are, in the standard way, 13 days before the modern calendar (in accord with the Julian Calendar used in Russia during Chekhov's lifetime, which was 12 days behind Western Europe when used in the nineteenth century and 13 days behind in the twentieth century).

Finally, although perhaps an uncommon confession, I am bound to say that I know there are mistakes here. I am not a professional linguist and Efros' meaning is sometimes very hard to interpret. But none of those acknowledged below are in any way responsible. All faults are entirely my own.

I have taken shameless advantage of my Russian friends to establish issues of copyright, of originality, and even of my right to re-publish the collection in this way.

The acknowledgements in a book are always the most enjoyable part of the process, and not only because it is one of the final tasks of the author or translator or editor. In this instance in particular there is nothing conventional about my appreciation and gratitude. This, however, is Nikolai Efros' book, and not mine, so there is more than presumption in lengthy acknowledgements, but first, many people have helped me translate and edit Efros' book – and second, on a personal note, this is a kind of Chekhovian 'swan song' for me.

First, I must thank Liliana Archibald for providing me with the original from the outset, and thus making it available to a much wider audience.

Then I must thank my sister, Irene Slatter (formerly of the Russian Department, Durham University) not just for her help with the translation, but also for her endless patience and support at a difficult time. It is with the deepest love that I salute her and our close friendship. Affection, gratitude and friendship must be expressed to my brother-in-law, Dr John Slatter (true historian, scholar and linguist, and recently retired from the Russian Department of Durham University). In spite of the fact that my inconsistency with the transliteration is clearly quite alien to him, he has been nothing but supportive and – as always to me – more than generous with his time.

I must also express appreciation to John Freedman and Robert Robertson who first accepted this project for Harwood Academic Publishers, and to those in the Drama Department of Goldsmiths College who awarded me a research grant but, more than that, gave me support and technical help, as well as criticism and advice. This particularly includes Robert Gordon, good friend, colleague and collaborator who, as often before, took the time to read and comment on this introduction; Hilary Wilson, former Administrator and old friend who came with me to an early meeting at Harwood, and had the unenviable task of teaching me 'Word'; David Smith for his word-processing skills, and Jacqueline Menzies for her practical help.

I am glad to acknowledge my friendship with Tatiana Shakh-Azizova and Aleksandr Akhtyrski, and to thank them with deepest gratitude for years of friendship, and professional help. A brilliant critic and true friend, Dr Shakh-Azizova no doubt underestimates how much I have learnt from her. Professor Aleksei Bartoshevich is also a much-respected friend for whom I have nothing but deep appreciation and affection. Likewise, Anatoly Smeliansky is and has been a generous friend and colleague, and I am glad of this chance to express my gratitude, my respect and my real enjoyment of his expertise, his amazing knowledge – and a shared sense of humour. I much appreciate what he has done in making this publication possible.

I am more than grateful to Richard Eyre (and for other help besides), Anatoly Smeliansky and Jean Benedetti for taking valuable time to comment on the cover – thus lending their support in advance of publication.

I should particularly like to thank the following: Brian Roberts, not only 'partner' but constant friend and source of support; Ruth Cohen for years of true friendship, fun and help Richard Saffron; Maggie Phelps; Rachel Summerson and Valentina Ryapolova, all of whom helped in various invaluable ways, as have others, such as Professor George Brandt – but lack of space does not permit me to name them all. Likewise, my Paris friends, Jacqueline Cahen, who helped me with the bureaucratic niceties of the Bibliothèque Nationale, and Patrice Pavis from whom I learned more over a cup of coffee than in hours in the library.

It has become a custom (and rightly so) to acknowledge help received from one's publisher and editor. I thank Diane Parker, Minh Ha Duong and Talia Rodgers of Routledge for their sorely tested patience and their practical support and help. There is particular pleasure in thanking Talia Rodgers for her friendship, sensitivity and faith. Few editors have had their patience so sorely tried by endless frustrating delays and interruptions – yet Talia always remained calm and confident. I thank her for making this project possible. I should also like to thank Sangeeta Goswami, Linda Paulus and the rest of the production department at Routledge for their patient rescheduling of publication deadlines.

I am deeply grateful to Dr Nick Worrall, formerly of Middlesex University, for enabling me to complete the Biographical Notes by sharing the load at short notice. His expertise has proved invaluable, and I am delighted to finally have this chance to work with someone whom I have always much respected and whose specialist knowledge is backed up with true scholarship. He too is not responsible for any errors or mistakes.

Finally, I should like to thank my nephew Paul Slatter – loved 'soul-mate' and young colleague – for his practical help. This translation and edition of Nikolai Efros' work is now finally accessible to the younger generation of Chekhov practitioners, scholars and students.

June 2004

PLAYS OF A.P. CHEKHOV AT THE MOSCOW ART THEATRE

Introductions by Vladimir Nemirovich-Danchenko and Nikolai Efros
with 198 illustrations

ALBUM
"RUSSIAN SUN"
No.7

M. Dobuzhinski 1914

1 A.P. Chekhov (Yalta, 1897).

The affinity between the Art Theatre and Chekhov was much greater than the general public realized. The relationship between Chekhov's artistic ideas and their influence on the theatre was so profound that they seem incommensurate with their brief duration.

You see, it really only lasted for about five-and-a-half years.

In the first year of the Theatre's[1] existence, Chekhov knew nothing of the Art Theatre, while in the Theatre very few people knew Chekhov personally. Others understood and loved him only after their own creative gifts had been harnessed to Chekhov's creative power. Then, after five years of work with the Theatre, he died. In this brief period such creative unity was consolidated that in today's Theatre [1914], there is scarcely a single serious rehearsal in which, for one reason or another, Chekhov's name is not mentioned.

Of course, this does not mean that with Chekhov the Art Theatre found an all-embracing theatrical style or form into which the works of other dramatists could be forced. If such a grave error ever occurred, then the reason was strictly temporary and transient, and resulted from the methodology acquired from Chekhov's plays and from the Art Theatre's admiration for the deep artistic meanings contained in his essential qualities as a dramatist: to liberate oneself from the conventional routines of theatrical customs and literary clichés; to return living psychology and ordinary speech to the stage; to look at life not only through its soaring peaks and deep crevices, life's highs and lows, but also through the daily life which surrounds us; to put an end to the theatricality of dramatic works, for so long emanating from the fanfares of special effects – a theatricality which for too long has given theatre over to the authority of that particular kind of craftsmanship which has repelled and antagonised its very life, alienated living literary talents and resulted in a kind of internal psychological death of live theatre.

The art of Chekhov is the art of artistic freedom and of artistic truth. It is the art of an artist who loved life all the more for his tenuous hold on it, given his illness. He loved the simple life given to everyone by God. He loved the birch trees and the sun-lit rays of a clear morning. He loved the meandering rivulets of the steppe 'which is enhanced by a pebble, just as eyebrows decorate the beautiful eyes of a girl'. He loved the soft whistling of a quail and the melancholy cry of an owl; light-hearted laughter; youth; naive faith; female love; literary friends; and he loved ordinary, unremarkable people from whom he derived gentle amusement. He loved the Russian language, its Slavic lyricism, its accurate contrasts and unexpected forms. And most of all, he loved 'to console his mind with dreams'.

He was sincere and spoke and wrote only as he felt.

He was deeply conscientious and spoke and wrote only about what he really knew.

He loved 'being', as only he could, living as he did as an 'artist-colourist', and he looked upon life with simple, clever eyes.

And from where – suddenly – did this melancholy come? The famous 'Chekhovian melancholy'[2] which so stunned the reader with the beauty of its subjective truth? As if from nowhere he instanta-neously and accurately revealed what each Russian intellectual carried in his heart. He illuminated what was closest to his reader's heart.

Where did this come from – so suddenly and mysteriously? From the illness which undermined his joy of living, or was it from his dreams of a better life?

The depths and seriousness of Chekhov's soul were never shared, even with those people closest to him. A deep and modest man, he liked concealment, and privacy of feelings and thoughts. But for all his reserve, sometimes – and particularly in his letters – he could not disguise his poignant longing for the simple joys of life within the reach of any healthy person. In the five years of his relationship with the Art Theatre, he was confined to the South – to the lacquered greenery of the Crimea which he disliked – and far removed from literary circles and the people he was close to; from the landscape of Levitan[3] and from Moscow – from all the sources for which he had particular affection – and he was often fretfully homesick. It is impossible to reread some of his letters without feeling moved:

> I am terribly bored. When I am working I don't even notice the day, but when evening sets in, then desperation comes. By the time you are playing Act II, I'm already lying in bed. I get up when it is still dark. Imagine it is dark, the wind blows and the rain beats on the window.

Yes, so there we have it. Imagine. At the very moment when Moscow appeared in his dreams (appeared in sparkling evening light), when the second act is playing in his favourite theatre – perhaps even when the second act of his *Three Sisters* in which Prozorov, struck in the provinces, wistfully says 'How I wish I could be sitting in Testov's restaurant'[4] – and when the audience are enjoying all the simple bless-ings of the capital while weeping over the fate of all those who are pining in the boring, melancholy backwoods – that is the very moment when the instrument of their tears, the author, is experiencing the despair of a prisoner. And when everyone he is thinking about is still asleep in the early morning, he is already getting up. And the wind howls and the rain beats on the window. And it is still dark.

I do not have the chance here to address most of the touching, affectionate or sad recollections which shrouded Chekhov's affinity with the Art Theatre. One of the writers who is most dear to our hearts, the 'collective artist' of the Theatre, has merged in quivering dreams and aspirations. For five years, by sheer chance, their lives were uniquely and closely interwoven, and created a movement in art which, in the history of Russian theatrical creativity, will never be forgotten.

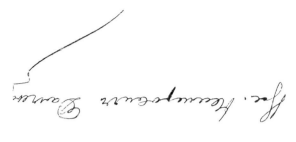

V.I. Nemirovich-Danchenko.

2 V. I. Nemirovich-Danchenko.

Pencil drawing by the artist A.A. Koiranski.

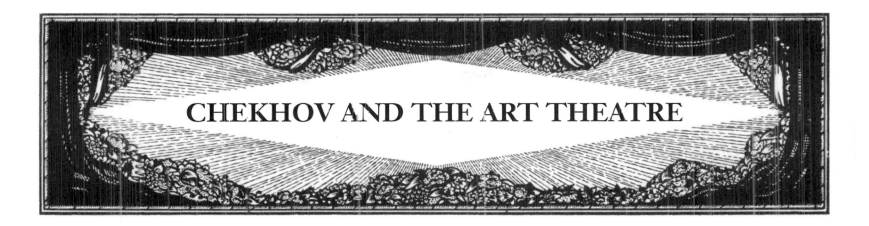

hekhov: truly the first love of the Art Theatre.

Like the very first time one falls in love with theatre itself, the heart cannot forget Chekhov.

The best pages do not yet cover a long period, but are already significant in the history of this Theatre – the most important part of its history, the most beautiful and touching, scattered with the tender light of poetry, fanned by sweet sadness. These pages depict the fascinating story of the five Chekhov productions which cemented the strong and noble connection between 'the Theatre of Chekhov' – as the Art Theatre was often called – and 'the playwright of the Art Theatre' as, with good reason, one might well describe the poet of *Seagull* and *Cherry Orchard*.

It was Chekhov's name which was the first to be uttered in the earliest discussion about the possibility of a public Art theatre, when the idea was still a far off and charming dream. And if and when anyone in the future starts to talk about the achievements of the Art Theatre, and what it has contributed to the world of Russian theatre, then again the first name which will unfailingly be mentioned would be that of Chekhov, and any discussion would have to be about these Chekhov productions.

In the same theatrical year in Petersburg[5] in which the poor *Seagull* was torn to pieces, when the author was so ridiculed that he was virtually hissed at, and when he fled from the Alexandrinski Theatre firmly vowing that he would never again write for the stage, Vladimir I. Nemirovich-Danchenko was also in Petersburg, receiving the Griboyedov Prize for the best play of the season for his own play, *The Prize of Life*.[6] The recipient so honoured, however, protested at the Jury's decision, and passionately declared the result which would have given him the greatest pleasure: 'I cannot accept this prize because – undoubtedly and without question – it is deserved not by my play, but by another. *Seagull* deserves it. That is the real diamond. That is the new pride of Russian drama. Since I do not wish to offend the honourable Jury, I must, however, concede in accepting the prize.' Nonetheless, V.I. Nemirovich-Danchenko remained firm in his opinion: *Seagull* 'is genuinely the pride of our drama. People do not see it yet, but soon everyone will understand.'

On 22 May 1897, starting off in a private room in the Slavianski Bazaar, and then moving on to Stanislavski's dacha, K.S. Stanislavski and V.I. Nemirovich-Danchenko talked without a break for 18 hours in succession. In the course of this discussion, stretching over a whole day and extending well into the night, the Art Theatre was born. In the discussion,

Chekhov's name was repeatedly mentioned if not by the one then by the other, each of whom shared the same artistic ideas and values as the other, and for both of whom Chekhov's name resounded like a clarion call for a new theatre, proclaimed like a military banner.[7] It would be an exaggeration to claim that the Art Theatre was created solely to perform Chekhov. But it would also be true to say that the Art Theatre became what it did because of the existence of Chekhov the dramatist, and was motivated by the need for a theatre of his own to realize his new kind of theatre – misunderstood as it was, and spoilt and rejected by the old theatre.

It was during a rehearsal of *Tsar Fiodor*,[8] produced for the newly created theatre, that without any warning, any advance notice, Chekhov stepped over the threshold of his 'home' for the first time. He entered and then...! And each time after he left, interested and delighted, he seemed unaware of how much love he took with him. And when illness chased Chekhov back again to [his] 'Devil's Island'[9] – to Yalta – he wrote to the director of the Theatre: 'The Art Theatre is the best page of the book which one day will be written about the modern Russian theatre. This Theatre is your pride, and is the only Theatre which I love – although I have not yet once been in it.'[10]

This is the first augury of the relationship between both parties, one which was to stretch throughout the whole life of the Art Theatre, and a blessing for both of the chief participants. On that unhappy night of 2 July 1904, with the tragedy at Badenweiler [Chekhov's death in the German spa, Badenweiler], those personal ties were severed. But the real relationship between Chekhov and the Art Theatre did not die that night. It remained permanent. That immortal part of the poet, incorporated in his beautiful creations, continues to live in this Theatre, and brings him to life: Chekhov's spirit hovers over Chekhov's house. Productions of Chekhov's plays are not simply a bright memory, or part of a fading past, but are actually a living presence in this Theatre. It is, of course, absurd to predict the future, to guess what lies far ahead,[11] but it will not be in the near future that this charming page will finally be turned over. 'They will still be writing about *Seagull* when you are no longer around', wrote Prince A.I. Urusov – one of the earliest admirers of Chekhov's plays, fresh from the impression made on him by *Seagull*, and notwithstanding the general lack of recognition for *The Wood Demon* (subsequently *Uncle Vanya*). The author of that letter could have said the same about the whole of Chekhov's theatre, about all of Chekhov's five great plays.

It is idle speculation to measure who has done the most: Chekhov for the Art Theatre, or the Art Theatre for Chekhov. In any case, without *Seagull*, without *Uncle Vanya*, and the challenges which they set for the Theatre *and* for the actor, there is no question that the Art Theatre would not be what it is; would not have found such a straight and immediate path to the attention, the heart and the love of its audience. But it is also undoubtedly true that without the Art Theatre, Chekhov would not have written *Cherry Orchard* and *Three Sisters* – at least not in the form of plays.

3 A.P. Chekhov (1902).

5

4 A.P. Chekhov (Yalta, 1901).

And no one can really know how long this poet's plays would have remained generally misunderstood if the Art Theatre had not broken down the prejudice circulating so strongly that even Chekhov himself believed it – believed that his work was unsuitable for the theatre and that he should have nothing to do with the stage. . . 'Oh, why did I start to write plays and not stay with short stories', Chekhov blurted out in one of his letters, written shortly after the catastrophic fiasco of *Seagull*'s premiere in Petersburg. 'Bits of the script went missing, lost out of carelessness, and with great hullabaloo and to absolutely no purpose.' This was not said out of temporary depression. His words express much more than simply the bitterness of pain and insult, and the complete lack of understanding. 'I was *ashamed, apologetic*' the author of *Seagull* wrote in another letter, around that time, to A.F. Koni.[12] And the letter continues: 'I left St Petersburg full of all kinds of doubts.' Those doubts centred increasingly and decisively on his inabilities as a dramatist; that he thought he had to completely give up writing for the stage, and leave it to those who 'were, in theatrical terms, less *clumsy*' than he thought himself as a playwright.

With the first production of *Seagull*, The Art Theatre in one stroke broke this absurd prejudice, gave Chekhov back to the Russian theatre, and gave him back his own faith in himself and confidence as a dramatist. Thus the Art Theatre really did do a great service to our (national) repertoire; it filled the abyss which had already begun to open up between theatre and life, and once again made theatre relevant, essential, meaningful and precious. Even if one were to exclude anything and everything else which Chekhov has done, then in this alone he has provided a great service to Russian theatre – and to Russian culture and society.

This decision, to shake the dust of the stage from his feet, was maturing in Chekhov and was, I think, a major tragedy for him as a writer. He was renouncing an area of creativity to which he had long been attracted and in which he was timidly beginning to test his strength as he recognised the writer in himself. I know that even as a young student he wrote and completed a complex and great drama in which the hero had the same name, Voinitski, as he then used again in *Wood Demon* and in *Uncle Vanya* [Efros is referring to *Platonov*].[13] Chekhov wrote a complex play, incorporating many ideas, and spent some considerable effort and energy on it, but as always Chekhov was the most severe and demanding critic of his own work, so he hid the play and, it seems, did not even baptise it with a title. So this very large notebook lay untitled and hidden in his desk. I do not know the content or the quality of this youthful Chekhov play which has now been lost to posterity.[14] That, however, is not really my point – what *is* significant and characteristic is that it demonstrates how early the future author of *Ivanov* was attracted to the theatre, and for how long he had been interested in writing plays. It was with that dream that Chekhov set out on his path as a writer – and it was that dream which he rejected completely after he suffered one failure after another in the theatre.[15]

Chekhov tried himself out as a playwright three times before [working with] the Art Theatre. And on all three occasions, the theatre and the audience were hard on him; after each of these three attempts – two in Moscow and one in Petersburg – he left the theatre embarrassed and distracted, even somewhat confused.[16, 17] Chekhov's letters are liberally scattered with disparaging references to his plays: 'my miserable little play', 'this bonbonniere play', 'the swine of (instead of *Ivanov*)' and such like. Yet it is permissible to wonder whether these disparaging and destructive references completely expressed what Chekhov really thought about his dramatic works to which the audiences had reacted so angrily. Chekhov liked to conceal himself and his real feelings behind a mask, as if he wanted to show other people that for him the plays were really just amusing trifles. Sometimes

6 A.P. Chekhov (Yalta, 1897).

the mask slipped and revealed the truth – the face of an author deeply saddened by being misunderstood. In one letter about that same *Ivanov*, supposedly only a 'bonbonniere play', and even 'accursed', he wrote: 'Whatever else, I do consider that my heroes are something new in Russian literature, and have not yet been approached in this way by anyone. The play is bad, but the characters are alive and not invented.' And then, with complete sincerity and without his usual disparagement, he confessed: 'I cherished a bold dream of encapsulating everything that has hitherto been written about the type of people who are bored and self-pitying, and through my *Ivanov* I tried to create a definitive portrait.[18] It seemed to me that all the Russian writers and dramatists who have felt the need to portray the character of such miserable whiners, have written automatically, without any specific form or viewpoint. My intention was to get away from that stereotype, even if I have fallen into the same trap myself.' And in another letter on the subject [he wrote]: 'I tell you honestly, sincerely, these people [he is referring to Ivanov and Dr Lvov] were born in my head – not from sea-spray; not from preconceived ideas; not out of an intellectual abstract; and not by chance. They are the result of observation and a study of life. They are the creations of my brain, and I feel that I have not lied by one centimetre, or exaggerated by one iota.'

5 A.P. Chekhov (Yalta, 1902).

This is really what lies hidden beneath the so-called 'amusing trifle', the 'pleasant amusement', as Chekhov described his plays in other letters. But it was this superficial view – until the intervention of the Art Theatre – that was held by the theatre-going public. The vast majority of Chekhov's audience did not understand what they were seeing, while the views and opinions of people like Prince Urusov were lost without trace. The audience already had a tender affection for 'Chekhov the short story writer'; the audience had read his books and accepted him as 'one of their own'. But between the loved and much-admired writer and his audience was the old, unreformed theatre, deaf and blind to the greatest beauties of Chekhov's plays. And the audience ceased to understand and excuse Chekhov, and turned away in anger. That old theatre ensured that the heroes of his plays were seemingly 'only idiots', as Chekhov himself had described the relationships in *Seagull*. The old-style theatre ensured that his play seemed 'silly, incomprehensible, even pointless', to return to the quotation from Chekhov's letter to Koni, quoted above. And the author left the theatre insulted and disappointed . . .

The first time this happened was at Korsh's Theatre where *Ivanov* was put on, I think at the end of 1888.[19] I remember this long-ago production fairly clearly – V.N. Davidov played Ivanov, and Miss Glama Meshcherskaya played Sara [Efros uses Sara's maiden name, and is referring to Anna, Ivanov's Jewish wife, formerly Sarah Abramson]. One or two things *did* please the audience at Korsh's premiere. During the whole of Act II, with the party at Lebedev's house, the audience laughed away merrily. While this is the least 'Chekhovian' act – the least characteristic of the new Chekhovian drama – it was accessible and people liked it. But the first act, the most beautiful one in *Ivanov* and, more important, the 'most Chekhovian' was quite beyond the attention of the majority of the audience. It did not arouse their feelings, and it did not involve them. In neither discussions of the play nor in contemporary reviews was there even a hint that in this first act of *Ivanov* a completely new way of writing plays had been born. But that is, in fact, the case and anybody who wants to analyse the method, the style and the internal meaning of Chekhov's creative development as a dramatist must, I think, pay particular attention specifically to the first act of this great Chekhovian drama. Here one can already find all the seeds of Chekhov's future as a dramatist. Here are all the tones, colours and moods of Chekhovian drama. Of course, this was completely unrecognised – it simply went unnoticed. The last act of the play, the denouement which Chekhov then reworked in vain, did at least make people angry and so Chekhov

7 A.P. Chekhov outside his dacha in Yalta (1903). With him are his beloved dogs.

had to put up with hissing and whistling at his dramatic debut. The first act was simply ignored. As members of the audience put it: 'It's a bit boring and one just can't understand what it's all about or what it's for.'[20] Ten years passed, and then this same act touched the soul of the audience with extraordinary force; today people listen to it with the deepest emotion and every word, every detail strikes a painful and sweet response in the heart of the audience . . .

The second time this happened was again in Moscow, at the very ephemeral theatre of Mrs Abramova (on the site of what is now Nezlobin's theatre).[21] And I remember that production also with great clarity. The author of the very *Ivanov* which had just failed at Korsh's Theatre risked a production of *Wood Demon*. The first night was 27 December 1889, but nonetheless in spite of the festive season, it drew only a small audience. Then there were five more performances of what was to be the first version of *Uncle Vanya* – a play which now almost never leaves the repertoire of several theatres – before it was consigned to the archives, never to return.[22] Weighed down by the negative criticism and anger which had greeted his drama, even Chekhov himself wrote that for him, 'it would be a real blow if some chance of fate took the play from its hiding place, and forced it to see the light of day'. Very few people discerned the beauties of this work, felt its depth and significance, and understood the mood contained in the play. Among these few was, again, Prince A.I. Urusov who, in his initial enthusiasm for *Wood Demon*, went so far as to rate it more highly than the new, reworked version which became *Uncle Vanya*, and even thought that the re-working of *Wood Demon* into *Uncle Vanya* had spoilt the original. Urusov expressed the tentative opinion that in the first version 'everything was more innovatory, bolder, more interesting'. But Urusov was alone in this view and in his enthusiasm. As one can read from any one of the theatre reviews of the period, the audience was angered and bewildered by the play. And almost equally angry were the newspaper critics who judged Chekhov's play disparagingly, even destructively. They wrote: 'Chekhov does not want to know the rules of drama, and can only tell a narrative on the stage.' Or: 'It is as if he has kept "minutes", not written a comedy.' The whole play, although trembling with feeling, only seemed to them artificially 'objective'.

In a letter about the fate of his second great play, Chekhov laconically described it in these terms: 'The newspapers criticized the actors for being sort of embarrassed.' Although much less perfect than *Uncle Vanya*, nothing truly Chekhovian – in which *Wood Demon* is rich – came across the footlights, or found an echo in the audience – largely, one would imagine, because it was absent from the stage in both the production and the acting of the drama.

The night-time conversation [Act II], now one of the most moving scenes in *Uncle Vanya*, became merely an absurd device by the author, seemingly just a stupid whim. And in the theatre the audience just giggled . . .

And then came the third attempt and great failure – this time in Petersburg, at the Alexandrinsky Theatre, which is where *Seagull* perished. Too much has already been written about this production and I don't need to dwell on it, even briefly; nor do I need to remind people how the audience, untouched and uninvolved by anything, began to laugh at the most inappropriate moments; responded once again with boredom, and criticized the author who, while of course a talented short story writer, was certainly not any kind of a dramatist – even though he definitely aspired to be a playwright and was trying in vain to get on the stage.

This was Chekhov in the theatre before the Art Theatre. It was essential to mention all of this, albeit briefly, in order to really emphasize the scale and significance of the complete about turn which we felt with the productions at the new Theatre. This Theatre, which had only just started, gave all of its strengths to *Seagull* – and the scene changed beyond recognition. Before this, the [contemporary] stage had been the barrier between Chekhov's plays and his audience. Now it was the stage which miraculously brought them closer; became the artistic intermediary between them; infused the play with its bright light and deep, subtle understanding; brought out the enormous sensitivity of the experience, and brought into the auditorium all the Chekhovian feelings – 'as tender as flowers' – and all the Chekhovian moods. The theatre had previously inflicted damage on Chekhov, but now it redeemed its guilt towards the poet by being immensely constructive. Chekhov was virtually reborn; Chekhov the dramatist was resurrected for the Russian public. There was no longer anybody who did not understand, who *still* misunderstood, or who remained indifferent. The Russian audience took first *Seagull* to its heart, and then, after that, the four other great Chekhov plays. As Prince Urusov stated: 'Moscow has definitely fallen in love with *Seagull*.' And he noticed the striking phenomenon of 'returning spectators' – those who came to *Seagull* 'several times in a row'. It could be that those who returned again and again came not merely to see the production, but also because they began to 'live' it. This is clarified by what Leonid Andreev[23] later wrote about another Chekhov play: 'We have ceased to be onlookers, ceased to be ourselves with our programmes and binoculars, but have turned into characters in the play.' These words are absolutely applicable to *Seagull* as well, and to all the Chekhov productions *en masse*. This is the miracle of what happened to Chekhov with the Art Theatre – a building 'small on the outside but huge on the inside'.

In this short introduction I must mention the story of the miracle which began on that memorable evening of 17 December 1898, the miracle described by V.I. Nemirovich-Danchenko – one of the creators of the first production – as 'the holy resurrection of Christ' or of the Art Theatre. Only I must declare one reservation: I am among those 'returners' described to Chekhov by Prince A.I. Urusov, but I was not, of course, at every single performance of Chekhov at the Theatre – performances which numbered more than 500 over 15 years. But I did see each play several times, many times, and attended every first night and the many revivals. My memory is not quite sharp enough to enable me to remember the distinguishing features and differences between every production of the same play.

8 A.P. Chekhov at his dacha in Yalta (1904).

Memories of different productions at different times are intertwined and I shall not try to separate them. What I shall do, is to describe each production as I remember it as a whole, except where in some cases there were such significant and thus memorable changes between the productions that they merit special mention – such as cast changes of the most important roles. After all, the main strength of all the productions, the strength of this rebirth of Chekhov on the Art Theatre's stage, consists not in separate performances, but in the entirety of their expression of the most treasured inner characteristics of Chekhov's works. Some performers were better, others worse; one could make many – and sometimes even considerable – objections to some of the acting, while one can only bow down in delight at the acting of others. But the main point is that there was always, as a constant feature identical to all of these hundreds of Chekhov performances, an authentic Chekhovian atmosphere, and the tender beauty and poetry of Chekhov's moods. It was because of this that the Art Theatre revolutionized the plays: it managed to capture them; it managed to understand them; it managed to appreciate them fully and to communicate them properly. 'That is what provided the harmony of performance, revealing the author's spirit in his most sacred intentions and characteristics, and the unforgettable impression of the performances.' It is curious that I am borrowing this quotation from an article by the very theatre critic – A.R. Kugel – who was not only one of the most opposed to the Art Theatre, but even its enemy; and who had unremittingly and powerfully criticised its work over the years . . .

And when, in order to write this essay, I had to summon up from memory, renew for myself the impressions which I had accumulated over a 15-year period, it was precisely my heart which remembered, which understood the Chekhovian moods and treasured characteristics; it was my heart which awoke and went to work. It is sometimes difficult – dimly, mistily – to free oneself from *individual* figures, individual scenes and theatrical images. The heart's memory speaks powerfully and audibly, involving and sweetly evoking this common mood.[24] I think that everyone who has tried to revive the experience of Chekhov's plays at the Art Theatre has the same feelings. And how can one possibly omit from this phenomenon the fulsome and crucial praise of the Moscow Theatre's production of Chekhov's *Seagull*? Is not this because they quite naturally really did understand and magnificently implement the work's essential qualities and characteristics?

I have already mentioned in passing V.I. Nemirovich-Danchenko, one of the initiators of the Art- 'Accessible' Theatre, who brought his enthusiastic love of Chekhov the dramatist to the

9 A.P. Chekhov (Yalta, 1902).

threshold of this Theatre, and rightly understood that this could be a fountain-head, a life source, from which the stage could be rejuvenated. When he was dreaming of creating a new theatre, it was Chekhov who always came to mind, and of course it was Chekhov and *Seagull* which came to the forefront of the repertoire. This was an extremely risky choice: a battle could have started with the audience over *Ivanov* or *Uncle Vanya*, the last of which had been reworked by then from *Wood Demon*, and with much greater chance of success. These Chekhov plays were nonetheless more acceptable to an uninitiated audience than *Seagull*, and particularly its first act. This brave choice is quite understandable: they wanted to submit their beliefs to the most powerful test, to ensure that its triumph would be all the greater. They wanted, without prevarication, to get down to the essence of Chekhov's dramatic work. If this faith was misplaced, then it was taking a hammer to crack a nut; if on the other hand it was the correct decision, then the work would have the consistency of Damascus steel. These admirers of Chekhov the dramatist bet everything on a single card: confident of holding the trump card, they were proved right in their conviction.

However, many obstacles had to be overcome, both internally and externally. The first of the problems which had to be resolved was K.S. Stanislavski's lack of understanding of Chekhov – and after all, it was Stanislavski who was to direct the production. In his memoirs of the first years

of the Art Theatre, Stanislavski himself writes with great honesty about his lack of sympathy at that time with the beauty of Chekhov's work.[25] He did not yet sense *Seagull*'s charm; could not yet see how it would engross its director; nor did he know either how to stage it or how to perform it as an actor. Like so many others, he too thought it was 'not for theatre' and that 'nothing would come of it'. He had to be convinced of its value by long discussions. Stanislavski then took the play away with him to prepare the production – but he took it without any faith. It was only much later, during the slow process of work on it that he became accustomed to Chekhov's work, and then he saw and understood everything, and once and for all fell in love with everything.[26] As both director and actor, the actor who created four charming and unforgettable characters from Chekhov's plays – namely, Astrov [*Uncle Vanya*], Vershinin [*Three Sisters*], Gayev [*Cherry Orchard*] and Shabelsky [*Ivanov*][27] – Stanislavski made an invaluable contribution to Chekhov theatre, to the treasure house of Russian dramatic art.

Chekhov too had to be won over, given his bad memories of the Petersburg production of *Seagull*, and his fear of experiencing the same fate again. 'It is the only Theatre I love', he wrote about the new Moscow Theatre. But in spite of loving it, he probably doubted whether even this Theatre would be able to transpose the beauty of *Seagull* to the stage. Perhaps he was already convinced that this was an impossibility. For some time Chekhov had turned down other requests to produce *Seagull*, a refusal motivated by the need to prove that any idea of putting it on would be a mistake and that 'he was *not* a dramatist' and there were 'so many good *real* plays'. Even before this, with reference to the publication of *Seagull*, he wrote: 'I am afraid that I shall soon be in a bad mood; Lavrov and Goltsev have insisted that *Seagull* be printed in *Russian Thought* and so now the literary critics will start to scourge me. This is repulsive – like stepping in a puddle in autumn.'[28] A theatre production threatened to bring even more unpleasantness. Chekhov, however, was unable to maintain his refusal for very long; he already loved this young Theatre so much, and saw in its success proof that both the public and the actors needed an 'intelligent theatre'. And so, with a quaking heart, frowning and angrily muttering to himself, Chekhov finally conceded – no doubt in the certainty that he would bitterly regret his concession. So it was with this sensitive background that the Moscow Theatre on the Karetni Ryad took such problems and responsibilities on its still new and unproven shoulders . . .[29]

But ahead lay even more significant achievements – successes not only given the context of the work, but also the very essence, the ideals, which motivated the work in the first place. On the one hand the Theatre relied almost exclusively on young, little-known and untried actors – actors who had not had time to develop, and had not yet acquired their skills and technique. This increased the challenge and the difficulties, but it also had an advantageous and positive side: the actors were still unformed, offering the possibility of plasticity, generosity, flexibility; their approach to acting was not yet ossified by stage tradition, and it meant that their approach to the realization of Chekhov in performance was open to innovation. There was almost never the need to overcome inertia or wean them away from inappropriate techniques or skills – simply because they didn't yet have any skills. By the same token, the actors did not have to be wrenched out of the jaws of routine or the chasm of tradition. This Theatre, and its acting, really was a blank page – a *tabula rasa*. This was immensely advantageous and repaid with interest any drawbacks from their lack of experience or confidence. I do not know whether this factor was given enough credit at the time but now, looking back over 15 years and considering the circumstances which initiated the first Chekhov performance, the advantages may be clearly stated.

The problem I have mentioned, however, emanated from a different direction. Chekhov had written his dramas,[30] and particularly *Seagull*, in a completely innovatory way. He was, of course, also concerned that his heroes should be distinctive and typical; he wanted his plays to represent a particular

10 A.P. Chekhov taking a kumys cure in Samara province, in 1900. [Kumys is fermented horse milk.] (From the photograph by Sredin.)

completed circle of action, and that the strands of the circle should be tied firmly together by an inner truth – a psychological necessity. But over and above this, he had another quite precise intention.

Given his artistic realism, Chekhov the dramatist did not sever links in any way with the basic tendency or characteristic of Russian literature nor, in particular, of Russian drama. The author of *Seagull* and *Uncle Vanya* is an artistic realist; no other term can be applied to him.[31] Chekhov worked from within the content of artistic realism, but considered that the content had not yet been fully developed, and that within the definitions of 'realism', of the re-creation of life, one could and should seize upon those other elements of life and the soul which could be found in the world around him. Chekhov understood that from defined and precise feelings, there is also a whole range of intermediate feelings: half-feelings, elusive and imperceptible shades, transitions, intermediate modulations. And from his own feelings and experience, he drew deeply and beautifully on those half-tones and half-feelings which comprise the atmosphere of life. Above all, he wanted to portray this in his dramas because his writer's soul particularly moved by these hidden psychological contours, these elusive experiences, and also because his artistic sensibility knew that there could be no truthful, authentic portrayal of life without such elements. What is beyond dispute is that if these 'half-tones' are removed from his representation, if this 'mistiness' is taken away, then one can only distort his creation, and the life and the characters portrayed in it.

And so when the old [traditional] theatre did just that – whether because it could not yet understand Chekhov and his style, or because it was actually incapable of handling these essentially unique attributes and innovatory Chekhovian techniques – his characters come over as dead, as two-dimensional and, in some ways which are hard to define, they appear underdeveloped and odd. It is not accidental that people found in *Seagull* 'just a collection of idiots'. The totality of his characters and the network of their interrelationships were lost and so failed to engage and move the audience. The result was that Chekhov did indeed seem to be 'not for the theatre' – but only because that theatre could not be Chekhovian.

That was the main challenge which faced the Art Theatre – otherwise it too would have shared its predecessors' fate in staging Chekhov's subtle dramaturgy. To sum up: it had to create the means of conveying 'moods'. This was not, of course, invented by Chekhov, nor was Chekhov the first to introduce 'mood' into dramatic poetry. It belongs to and is inherent in every truly poetic work; and it is possible to demonstrate moments – even in such conventional drama as Ostrovsky's[32] – where everything is dependent on the 'mood'. But Chekhov provides a dominating emphasis and significance to this element: it becomes *the* essential prerequisite for staging the plays.

Moreover, the Art Theatre had no real 'precedent' to follow. As far as the director was concerned [Stanislavski], it is well known that the Art Theatre was profoundly influenced by 'Meiningen principles'[33] although it became in many ways more subtle as this influence was filtered and diluted.

The success of the 'Meiningen principles' was evident in the first production of the new Theatre, in *Tsar Fiodor*.[34] Stanislavsky was evidently influenced by 'Meiningen principles' in his productions of both historical and contemporary plays – not least, for example, in [Tolstoi's] *The Power of Darkness*.[35] But if this Meiningen approach had been applied to a Chekhov play it would, of course, have been damaging. The Meiningen approach suited the Art Theatre *initially* in that it pared away anything theatrically extraneous, but this was only the basis of a negative virtue. An intense and exciting search began, driven by the need for a particular sensitivity to, and depth analysis of, the sense and meaning of Chekhov's work. Chekhov was a new kind of realist – and the theatre of Chekhov had similarly to find a 'new realism'. With one stroke, Chekhov painted an innovatory light on the whole picture; the Theatre had to learn how to use these dramatic techniques, to search out those specifics which would clarify and illuminate the meaning and atmosphere of the whole.

11 A.P. Chekhov (Yalta, 1897). (Photo by Sredin.)

Of course, you remember the audience's noisy reaction and derisive laughter; their derisory response to the flapping curtain [in *Seagull*]; to the sound of the crickets; the clattering of horses' hooves on the wooden bridge, and so on and so on. Or the assumption that the Art Theatre wanted to replace a sense of real people with naive effects; wanted only to amuse the audience with cheap naturalism – with stage tricks. So went the numerous attacks on the play. But this was simply a total lack of understanding. Those were the responses of people who could not see the wood for the trees. It is not the curtains, moving in the wind, or the cricket behind the stove which were essential and effective when the Art Theatre produced Chekhov, and was searching for the appropriate techniques to truly express the play [*Seagull*]. Nor was it *an und für sich* [for its own sake].[36] The Art Theatre was not about such childishness. In fact, these were just a means to an end – ends which turned out to have validity, and which created reality. So if the sound of the crickets conveyed the mood of that moment more fully and powerfully when heard in that miserable and desolate room where Uncle Vanya and Sonia sit – then, yes, they used cricket sound effects to enhance the production. Or in order to truly convey the evocative significance of departure, then this could be readily obtained through the sound of horses' hooves on a bridge. These were evocative methods which were woven into the total *mise en scene*. And they gladly utilized this method as an aid to creating atmosphere and mood.[37] It has been argued that it is the actor alone who makes theatre – a rather arrogant and exaggerated claim. Even the theatre of the older generation of actors was not solely reliant on character portrayal. So if it proved impossible to limit theatre only to the actor in the old drama, still less is it possible in the new Chekhovian drama.

Of course, these methods were only a part of the whole – the centre of gravity, even with the new drama, still emanated from the actor, from the actor's communication of emotions, his [sic] way of being and speaking on stage. Chekhov's words, with their 'implicit meaning' (which could not fail to move one), also required a new way of delivering them. The whole economy of the spectacle was increased in import by silent action, by pauses, by interruptions in the dialogue [Efros is implying subplot]. This was essentially dictated by the very essence of Chekhovian drama, and the Art Theatre fully understood, valued and realized all of these new techniques of stage art.

12 A.P. Chekhov and the Moscow Art Theatre artist [actor] A.R. Artem in a schoolteacher's uniform. (Photo by Vasilevski.)

13 A.P. Chekhov (Yalta, 1904) [sepia]: (Photo by Sredin.)

But in order to utilize and realize the techniques properly, it was essential to throw out all the conventional means of conveying emotion on stage. Stanislavski's hatred of clichés – which motivated his whole theory of stage acting, his 'system' and all those whose acting he influenced – developed out of Chekhov's plays, and without Stanislavski even realizing it. This 'system' was not yet consciously articulated, but it was already alive and motivating the work on stage when Chekhov's plays were produced and acted. Chekhov's plays demanded 'a return to Shchepkin' – which subsequently became the Art Theatre's slogan.[38]

Beginning with *Seagull*, the Art Theatre started to implement all of this, and although it was not perhaps initially fully realized, it was always done with a confidence which then in turn created a miracle – with 'our programmes and binoculars' we ourselves became participants in the performance. We became 'the characters'.[39] It is here that the real charm of a Chekhov performance in the Moscow Theatre lies: there is charm, there is artistic significance, and there are essential principles. The performances acquired an extraordinary allure and attraction. Since the old theatre had ceased to speak to the 'collective soul', society had already become indifferent to the theatre – but now people returned to theatre, and identified with it again. The gulf between society and theatre disappeared. A few years ago, the response was that the success of the Art Theatre was just a passing fad. But a fad, or fashion, does not last for years – it is capricious and transient, and what occupies our thoughts is rapidly trampled into the dust under our feet. Given how clearly one may see the real and profound reasons for the Art Theatre's success in Chekhov's plays, and Chekhov's triumphs in the Art Theatre, any mention of 'fashion' belongs in the dust of polemics.

The evening of 17 December 1898 arrived. The Art Theatre preserves this memory carefully and tenderly, and these reminiscences are moving. However, I believe that the evening lives on also in the memory of those who were at the performance just as spectators. I don't know if I have a theatrical memory which is particularly brighter, stronger, clearer or more meaningful than others, although my memory does preserve many extraordinary performances from various theatres. The same Art Theatre has shown us the decorative scenery of Dobuzhinski in [Turgenev's] *A Month in the Country*, and the scenography of Alexander Benois,[40] and before then, the scenery of *Seagull*'s first act seems not just modest in its charm, but even perhaps rather miserable in the eyes of those who have been very spoilt, or who have developed considerable expectations over the years. To avoid repeating myself later, I must say the same about the old, grey landowner's house, with its white columns, in the first act of *Uncle Vanya*; or about the cherry orchard which can be seen through the window, bathed in white light, in Chekhov's 'swan song', or about the 'immense horizons' in the second act of that same *Cherry Orchard*, and so on. It is justified that the Art Theatre wanted the visual aspects completely redone when it intended to bring *Seagull* – its first Chekhov production – back into the repertoire from which it had been accidentally dropped. But even with the first design of *Seagull*, the necessary mood or moods were created by the distant lake, the white curtain flashing mysteriously, or the unearthly lights of the play-within-the-play – and it put one in the necessary mood or atmosphere just as other kinds of decor did in subsequent acts and productions of Chekhov's plays. These features were silent, dead in a material sense, but made an important contribution to the life of the whole production.

I vividly remember the anxiety which seized me when I saw the picture

14 A.P. Chekhov in his study in Yalta (1903). The mantelpiece has an inset panel painted by Levitan. [See Biographical Notes.] (Photo by Sredin.)

15 The armchair in which Chekhov read the newspaper every morning. Reading them one after the other, he usually put them down in a big heap to his right. Once, when he glanced at them, he said: 'When in heaven God asks me why I wrote so little, I will say I used to read newspapers!' On the round table by the door are photographs of actors and actresses. Often noticing that guests would examine these photographs, A.P. [Chekhov] would say: 'What a fine actress V.F. Kommissarzhevskaya is.' Her portrait in various poses, was on display there. (Photo by Sredin.)

through the parted curtains, that sad framework for 'the plot of a short story'.[41] And my anxiety – for at that moment there was only anxiety – grew worse all the time, with each sentence spoken on stage, and with every move from the actors. As we now know, on the other side of the footlights they were acting with deathly feeling, while on this side of the footlights many hearts were beating with a different but equally powerful fear. The reason was because what was happening to them and to us was something completely new, incomprehensible, still nameless and undefined, but it was already engaging – promising a new sadness and new joy for some of us. As Prince A.I. Urusov formulated it in his impressions of *Seagull*: 'For whole minutes long it seemed that life itself was speaking from the stage.' This was, and is, always the way people describe every successful theatre show. But on this occasion those words really meant something different, and the life which was being spoken from that stage was somehow quite different – as if it had a thinner veneer, and as if in revealing its soul, it communicated a precious content.

Of course, nobody in the audience realized any of this yet; at the time, no one understood what was happening, that anything was amiss – or what sort of miracle was taking place, but a miracle *did* take place, and cast its spell over us. In describing this fear, I think I have truthfully defined the audience's mood at the start of this performance. Of course, in the midst of this fear there were those who sat with indifference, or mocked, and refused to be affected by what was pouring across the stage to the audience. There was more than enough in the performance which was unusual, which had never been seen before or since, yet there were a few people who reacted badly, and bristling with anger, denounced the whole thing 'as a plot'. As the first interval revealed, they were, of course, only a minority. Yet it is also undoubtedly the case that those involved in the production were themselves slightly embarrassed: Masha's snuff box embarrassed them; likewise Medvedenko's long, unhappy speech. They were embarrassed when Trepliov spoke of his mother's jealousy of some woman called Zarechnaya [Nina] It was more than embarrassment – there was a mixture of irritation, pain, sadness. This grew all the greater when Nina began to speak in a way that people on stage never speak – drawlingly, like a refrain, came: '. . . people, lions, eagles and pheasants, reindeer with horns . . . all life, all life, all life.' [Act I, Trepliov's play].[42] At that moment, the new poetry had very few disciples, and was the object of jokes and ridicule. It really was a risky and dangerous moment in the Act, and in those seconds it seemed to me personally that *Seagull* would perish once more.

And yet as time passed, the mood became somehow thicker, more powerful. Scattered around were 'temples' of implication, of hidden meaning, of things 'not completely felt', if this neologism is permitted – the neologism or novelty needed when Chekhov's performances are discussed – and gradually began to collect into some harmonious entity, albeit as yet unclear. The emotion was becoming that of artistic joy – and triumph. When Masha, so ugly and sniffing snuff, was left alone with the ageing but still handsome Dorn, hardly able to hold back the sobs in her throat, tremblingly starts to say: 'Help me. I will do something silly. I will make a mockery of my own life'

16 Artists of the Moscow Art Theatre, visiting Chekhov in Yalta (1900), with the production of his *Seagull*. Standing (from right to left): M. Gorki (staying with Chekhov at this time), A. Vishnevski, A.P. Chekhov, K.S. Stanislavski, V.I. Nemirovich-Danchenko, Artem; seated in the front row (from right to left) Knipper, Lilina, Raevskaia, Luzhski; front row (on the ground) Meyerhold, Alexandrov, Sanin, Moskvin, Tikhomirov. (Photo by Vasilevski.)

The main defect was in the representation of Trepliov on stage. All the lyrical ambivalence was removed from this character by Mr Meyerhold's performance. This character has been poisoned and injured by life, yet it was not grief which came over – but petty insults, and irritation. The actor Mr Meyerhold interpreted him, moreover, without any stage presence or infectious charm. Meyerhold's performance as Johannes Vockerat in Hauptmann's *Lonely Lives* [sic – *Einsame Menschen*, 1891][44] was callous and without any charm – and this was even more the case with Trepliov. So the audience remained indifferent and cold to this Chekhovian hero, and instead of loving him, felt sorry for him – something the author of *Seagull* had scarcely expected.[45]

There was too little tenderness, dreaminess, or joy of life in Mrs Roksanova's performance of Nina Zarechnaya. This young actress – who

17 Actresses of the Moscow Art Theatre in the year of the first production of *Seagull*. Seated: Petrova, Lilina, Knipper, Raevskaia. (Photo by Vasilevski.)

– and then immediately dissolves into sobs through which we can barely hear: 'I love Konstantin' – there, on the garden bench, slightly to the right of us centre-stage, there the emotion and mood had finally been formulated, and taken on complete confidence. Then we the audience were completely won over by the power of Chekhov and the Art Theatre. New feelings arrived which were previously unknown in the theatre, a new enthusiasm had shaken our very being, and Chekhov in the theatre was instantly and irreversibly confirmed. So the Art Theatre had won. It was able to implement the work, to produce Chekhov on the stage, and convey to the audience everything Chekhovian in its entirety, richness, and subtlety.

My memory lets me down when I try to recall the contribution made by individual actors other than as a general impression. Now I will look at the whole performance of *Seagull*, and not just Act I. Not all the actors were equally successful. It was only much later that Stanislavski mastered his role as Trigorin; initially he was too 'meek', weak-willed, and played up the dandy too much.

Many years later, remembering that first *Seagull*, K.S. Stanislavski told me: 'I knew nothing of the literary world [of Trigorin]. I had no imagination, no idea about life, nor the daily lives of those kinds of characters in the literary world. And so Trigorin seemed to me quite different from the way Chekhov had written him.'

In the second production of *Seagull* [1905][43] there was little which was generally new or improved, except that Stanislavski reworked his Trigorin, and partly in line with the author's own oblique, laconic but significant directions. Stanislavski lost some of his earlier misinterpretations. Rising to new heights, he gave us 'the writer' which was missing from his Trigorin in the first performance.

18 Group of Moscow Art Theatre actors (1899). From left to right: Luzhski, Nemirovich-Danchenko, Alexandrov, Sanin, Stanislavski. (Photo by Vasilevski.)

shortly afterwards left the Art Theatre ensemble – had great confidence, and was able to convey her feelings, but she was neither tender, nor naïve, nor the lovely girl from the other side of the lake. All the poetry of a first love affair, of a first 'dream', was missing from her performance. In the last act, when Zarechnaya has now become an actress, when she has already been broken by life – when infidelity in love has revealed the darkest side to her – the feelings of grief and mourning became unnecessarily morbid, even hysterical. Such feelings were inappropriate to the Chekhovian. I must add that in the second production, when Mrs Lilina started to play Nina Zarechnaya, this Chekhovian character was still not completely successful – even today it has remained badly played in Chekhov's theatre. Of course, both Mr Meyerhold

19 Model for Act I of *Ivanov*, designed by V. Simov.

20 A.P. Chekhov in Yalta, at his dacha (May 1904). [This was two months before his death.] [Sepia.] (Photo by Sredin.)

21 Programme of the first production of *Seagull*.

and Mrs Roksanova had good moments, and in spite of serious defects, the main point is that nonetheless they maintained the crucial element of Chekhov's spirit: they never damaged those vital aspects of the general structure and overall mood of the play.

The other participants in this memorable production were much luckier. While strongly welded into a single unit, they individualized their characters excellently. Each of them was completely free of theatrical clichés; each found new colours which hitherto had been unavailable to the actors' palette; each of them found new, original, warm and tender tones. I don't know whether they found it for themselves, it was found for them, or the directors created it, but those characters were there, and they utterly charmed us. Those actors were Mrs Knipper as Arkadina; Mr Vishnevski as Dorn; Mr Luzhski as Sorin; Mr Tikhomirov as Medvedenko and – *prima inter pares* [sic: first among equals] – Mrs Lilina as Masha, who was the best actor in the production.[46]

These impressions became stronger as the performance continued, although slightly weakened during Act II. Everyone in the audience was shaken by Act IV. When 'the glass of ether broke' – when Dorn took Trigorin to one side, and interrupting some invented line, said in a muffled voice: 'The fact is, Konstantin Gavrilovich has shot himself' [see p.25, Illustration 45] – the audience was struck with tremendous force. There were no longer any

sceptics left. No one mocked the play any more. Instead, everyone was full of that joy which in art goes hand in hand with feelings of grief.

The Rubicon had been crossed. The Art Theatre had now become irreversibly Chekhov's theatre.

The second Chekhov show was *Uncle Vanya*, on 26 October 1899. This production was anticipated like a holiday. Partly perhaps because it did not have the same stormy success as *Seagull*, a success which passed quickly – and so it was actually *Uncle Vanya* which became the best-loved of all Chekhov plays at the Art Theatre. For the Art Theatre company, the staging requirements of the play were in general the same as for Chekhov's debut for the Art Theatre, while the resolution of the practical problems were essentially the same as with *Seagull*, only more subtle and perfect. Since the Theatre now had a precedent, there was greater certainty and the same brave artistic courage. Given this, I don't need to describe the over-all character of the play's production or the general structure of performance, and would only repeat myself. One may judge the results by returning to the opinion of Mr Kugel, quoted above [page 8] and which directly relates to *Uncle Vanya*. In my opinion Mr Kugel's views are significant in coming from one of the opponents of the Art Theatre and not an enthusiast – among other criticisms, he was indignant about the Art Theatre's 'dead things', and critical of the directors' imagination and discipline. Imbued in this play was all the Chekhovian melancholy, and in giving it full and beautiful expression on stage, it in turn imbued the audience, and held it in its sway. In its integrity of mood, *Uncle Vanya* is perhaps the best of Chekhov productions at the Art Theatre.

The individual performances in *Uncle Vanya* were undoubtedly much greater than in *Seagull*. There were almost no failures here, and none of the characters was reduced in artistic significance or in their considerable charm, while there were other performances which truly were a degree higher in perfection – above all, Mr Stanislavski's Astrov, Mr Artem's Waffles [Telegin], and Mrs Lilina's Sonia. I don't know how many times I saw them over the years, and every time I was seized by their utter charm. Virtually as successful, almost as 'whole', as truthful, as bright, and yet at the same time understated in the Chekhov style, were Mrs Knipper's Elena, Mr Luzhski's dried-up Professor Serebriakov, and others. I was always left a little dissatisfied with

22 Model for Act I of *Uncle Vanya*, designed by V. Simov.

24 Stage in the Pushkin Theatre (outside Moscow), where rehearsals were held for the first Moscow Art Theatre Chekhov productions. (Photo by Vasilevski.)

23 Programme of the first performance of *Uncle Vanya*. [Age and print overlay have damaged the image.] (Photo by Vasilevski.)

Uncle Vanya himself – Mr Vishnevski played him with many excellent details, but somehow it did not come over with the essential unified tone – a tone or note which made Voinitski particularly dear to Chekhov himself. There is some kind of psychological flaw in his nature, in Uncle Vanya's feelings of emptiness, of bitterness. I must also mention Mrs Samarova [Marina] whose role, although small, contributed greatly to the completeness, charm and expressiveness of the last scene of the play. The house is empty again, the noisy Petersburg guests have left and, amidst the surrounding sadness, there is one consolation: 'We shall rest, Uncle Vanya. We shall see diamonds in the sky . . .' [Sonia, see illustration 73, page 38]. I don't think anyone who has ever seen this scene at the Art Theatre, who has heard its final chord, will ever forget it. One need only touch on this theatrical memory to tap into a whole range of both sad and sweet memories. . .

The Art Theatre ended its second year with *Uncle Vanya* playing to almost universal acclaim and affection. 'I am not ashamed to admit,' Leonid Andreev wrote, 'that while I am in love with this Theatre's present – I am even more in love with its future.' These feelings were shared by the best of Moscow, and the main source of these loving feelings were the two Chekhov plays of which I have spoken only briefly.

That spring the Art Theatre set off for the South to show itself to its author whose illness stopped him from coming to Moscow. The Moscow joke had it that 'the mountain has gone to Muhammad'. At a distance they had been acquaintances; now they could become closer and some strong personal

friendships developed which were only broken by that night in Badenweiler [with Chekhov's death]. Of course, the Art Theatre people started to say that Chekhov had to reverse his decision about not writing for the theatre any more, and had to give 'his Theatre' a new play.[47] In conversations, Chekhov sometimes made some vague hints about a future play – but so vague that it was impossible for them to deduce anything other than the fact that Chekhov *might* write a play. Convincing Chekhov to write a new play, trying to wring one out of him, just getting him to make a decision, all took a long time but was of the utmost importance. Eventually the Theatre received thin sheets of paper, thickly covered with tiny handwriting. These were the first two acts of the new play which Chekhov himself called 'a light comedy'. I know that these two acts left the Theatre only with a vague impression. The true significance of this work had not been understood as yet, and they had to wait a long time for the rest of it. The Theatre was upset, almost despairing. Finally A.P. Chekhov arrived in Moscow in person, and handed over the rest of the play. This was *Three Sisters* – performed on 31 January 1901. And a third play, no less beautiful, was added to the two existing Chekhov productions.

I missed the premiere for completely accidental reasons, and the only time in all the years in the life of my favourite Theatre. So I cannot personally convey how the audience responded, or the extent to which the audience sensed the play's extremely upsetting tone. It was reported that one could feel a certain coldness in the auditorium, and that the audience was not completely taken by the play. I don't know why this would have happened, and cannot explain it given that there is everything in the play to capture and captivate any audience.[48]

Anyway, when I was present at the most recent performance of *Three Sisters*, not only was there no coldness, but on the contrary – the audience sat completely captivated and charmed, at one with the stage action. In the last act I was not alone in sitting with tears in my eyes, and the sound of sobbing was heard from several parts of the theatre: that was when the music of the march was heard as the regiment left, when Masha spoke about the curved sea-shore, and when Tuzenbakh came to say goodbye.

'I have seen life', Leonid Andreev wrote after seeing a performance of *Three Sisters*, and he confessed: 'It excited and tortured me, filled me with suffering and sorrow – and I am not ashamed of my tears.' And the same witness of *Three Sisters* at the Art Theatre continued: 'The grey mass of

25 Model for Act III of *Three Sisters*, designed by V. Simov. [Sepia.]

26 Model for Act III of *Uncle Vanya*, designed by V. Simov.

humanity was shaken, and seized by a single unifying powerful feeling in being faced with other people's human suffering . . .

'People come to the theatre to enjoy themselves, but in this Theatre something else has happened to them: the whole detritus of petty personal woes, of vulgarity and misconceptions, have all been thrown out.' Pouring out of this play is the longing for a better life, a beautiful life, cleansed of its current pettiness, of the great and small injuries of life. This work is simultaneously both deeply sad and profoundly joyous. And it incorporates something new in Chekhov's work – a seed of optimistic faith. Both the melancholy and the faith are powerfully communicated to anyone who has ever see *Three Sisters*.[49] People could laugh as much as they wanted at 'To Moscow! To Moscow! To Moscow'. Or parody it. But it reverberated for most people, and for long afterwards it resounded like a clarion call. I will allow myself just one more quotation from that same excited and lovely 'review' by Leonid Andreev: '. . . like a ray of sun from behind a cloud, like a golden thread, this clarion call penetrates the grey gloom, and lives on invincibly in the three female hearts' – and with them, it lives on in any Russian heart which yearns for a better life.

This is an overview of the nature of Chekhov's third play, a general impression. But to be more specific: the individual performances of the actors were beautiful. In order to list all the lucky performers on the stage of *Three Sisters*, I would have to write a very long roll-call, and that is because both the main and the subsidiary parts were all played with great charm, fidelity, expressiveness and effectiveness. It is the richest of Chekhov's plays in the number of characters, and with the most insignificant of exceptions, all of the characters – from Vershinin and Masha down to Ferapont and Fedotik – were all superbly played.

Only the blind, or those opponents with deliberately averted or closed eyes, could claim that the Art Theatre lacked a whole collective of good actors – and particularly given that the director and his 'unifying will' had captured them. It was in *Three Sisters* that a whole ensemble of fine actors gave their best interpretation and character-creation. Mrs Knipper had never before been so powerful as in her playing of Masha, particularly in her last scenes. Except as Fraulein Bensch in *Kramer* [Hauptmann's *Michael Kramer*].[50] Mrs Lilina has never reached such heights of stage artistry and creativity as she did in the role of Chekhov's Natasha – a performance complete and brilliant in every detail. And perhaps never before has the Art Theatre's and the public's main idol, the primary object of the audience's sympathy and joy, been so artistically perfect and deeply lyrical as Mr Kachalov was as Tuzenbakh. As for the part of Vershinin – if not *the* best, then it is one of the best achievements of Mr Stanislavski. In my opinion, these four gave the best performances of the production, but equally memorable are Mrs Savitskaya as Olga; Mrs Andreeva as Irina; Mr Artem as Chebutykin; Mr Luzhski as Andrei; Mr Vishnevski as Kulygin; Mr Gribunin as Ferapont; Mr Moskvin as Rode – and a few others who I now can't remember.[51] In my view, I might criticize the production for a few oddities, but they were purely external. In the sum of its parts and in the individual parts there was and is nothing to criticize – it warrants only homage. Chekhov achieved a complete victory with this third attempt. Even if it was not appreciated immediately (in that the first performance was not an instant triumph), both appreciation and triumph were not long in coming, and confirmed *Three Sisters* as the jewel in the Art Theatre's crown.

Chekhov no longer needed to be persuaded to write for the theatre: the results of such perfect staging ensured that his dramatic creations had taken flight. Many dramatic plans were hatched – with *Cherry Orchard* barely

completed, we now know, after all, that Chekhov was already beginning to think of a new drama, a drama which was to centre on a scholar who, deceived in love, left to do scientific research in the far north.[52] To the great grief of the Russian theatre, [Chekhov's] death was all too imminent and such plans went with him to the grave . . . Soon after *Three Sisters*, Chekhov did what he had always done – in conversations with Stanislavski and other members of the Art Theatre he began to make vague hints about his new play. These oblique hints contained flashes of a plot: through an open window was a large orchard belonging to a landowner and through that window one could see cherry trees, picked out in white light; someone was playing billiards; an old servant wandered around an old house; a woman, at first quite old and then much younger, had lost her money . . . . *Cherry Orchard* was developing in the poet's soul – a sad 'farewell' to a past which was receding, and a joyful welcome to a coming future. Chekhov guarded the title of this new play jealously, even keeping it from his wife who was lying ill in bed[53] until finally he just whispered it in her ear, not daring to say it aloud, while he wouldn't even whisper it to his sister but wrote it on a piece of paper and told her to read it for herself. Eventually, he had to give up both the secret title – and the play itself. A large exercise book of thick post office paper was sent to the Art Theatre, and on 17 January 1904 – the author's name day – *Cherry Orchard*

27 Programmes for the Moscow Art Theatre touring productions (Berlin, Vienna, Prague). (Photo by Vasilevski.)

28 Model for Act III of *Seagull*, designed by V. Simov.

was premiered. To the three existing miracles a fourth was added, and just as beautiful and charming. Chekhov's writing of *Cherry Orchard* was even more subtle and tender than the previous plays – the drama scented as sweetly as its title.

Thousands of threads connect the soul of a poet to his homeland, and through these threads are transmitted all the concerns of his country and compatriots. The coming of spring was already felt in the last winter frosts, and however removed from 'politics', this could not fail to be reflected in *Cherry Orchard*.[54] With a characteristically Chekhovian 'chord', these new notes resounded subtly in the play. While Chekhov always became angry when defined as a pessimist, with *Cherry Orchard* he had the right to become particularly angry. In this play there was no character now saying that one day 'we will see the sky sparkle with diamonds' [Sonia in *Uncle Vanya*, see illustration 73], nor did the characters say with a sigh that 'in two or three hundred years, life would be beautiful' [*Three Sisters*]. Here there is complete confidence that we are planting a new and beautiful orchard. And the scenic requirements of this new play set the Art Theatre a rather different task in staging the play: it would not properly express Chekhov's play if these new notes were not clearly communicated. Were I to be asked exactly how or where these new features may be found in the play – I would be unable to illustrate them since they are imperceptible, but they were present in the play.[55] These features suited the general mood and atmosphere [of the time]. *Cherry Orchard* was more cheerful than the preceding three plays: in it was a kind of pre-dawn freshness. As for the tears in Act III, prompted by the news

that the cherry orchard has been sold – those tears were not at all similar to those prompted by the march music as the regiment leaves with Vershinin [*Three Sisters*]; or motivated by the line 'They've gone' from *Uncle Vanya*, or the feelings, like fragile, delicate flowers, in *Seagull* aroused by 'Remember, Kostia' [Konstantin].

Then it was not that the cherry orchard had been sold and cut down, but that the orchard in Anya's and Petya Trofimov's young dreams would flourish – a new and beautiful one. But now you look at the 'cherry orchard' mournfully, and with a new feeling of insult to the soul. That feeling was not current then [in 1904], because it was not only Petia Trofimov who believed in it, and waited . . .[56]

When you dismantle the beautiful entity of the *Cherry Orchard*, and visualize the individual characters, then it is Gayev, played by K.S. Stanislavski, who takes first place. Chekhov wanted Stanislavski to play Lopakhin, the character Chekhov particularly valued as central to the play. I think he did not regret the fact that Stanislavski rejected Lopakhin[57] and instead played that 'grown-up child' Gayev, given how perfectly he created the character: his performance of this adult but naïve child was both noble in comic terms, and yet also touching, and – like Firs – the whole audience loved him tenderly. Mrs Knipper [as Ranevskaya] hit just the right notes, preserving the hollowness and sweetness of her character, and she easily and without any exaggeration conveyed 'the light drama' of tears through laughter – and laughter through tears. In his brightly comic role of Yepikhodov, Mr Moskvin created his best part to date, and an exemplary theatrical parody. It was said that the actor

29 Lunch at F.K. Tatarinova's in Yalta: Moscow Art Theatre Company visiting A.P. Chekhov (1900) with the production of *Seagull*. (Photo by Gusev.)

actually gave something of himself to the very text of the play – so much so that at rehearsals, Chekhov retained some of Mr Moskvin's highly successful improvisations. In Mr Kachalov's performance as the outwardly ridiculous old student, Trofimov, all the beauty of his inner being, and of his young optimism, came shining through, and his rigour was mixed with subtle tenderness. Perhaps Mrs Lilina's Anya was not as young as the author had intended, but nonetheless she conveyed immense sincerity and simplicity of feeling. And perhaps there was a certain inaccuracy and inconsistency in Mrs Andreeva's Varya, but this was redeemed by a touching performance.

Perhaps Lopakhin, as played by Mr Leonidov, did not come over the way Chekhov had imagined him, but his forceful playing of the end of Act III reconciled us to the performance as a whole. Among other successful aspects of the production one must also mention Chekhov's favourite, Mr Artem, irreproachable as Firs; Mrs Muratova as Charlotta, and Mr Alexandrov as Yakov [Yasha].

The audience went home utterly charmed after the premiere of *Cherry Orchard*, but this was also their first personal encounter with their favourite writer – an encounter which was used to honour him publicly. This was the feast before disaster struck: a few months later, and those who stood to applaud *Cherry Orchard* and its author then stood by an open grave at the Novodevichi Monastery. . .[5] The fifth of Chekhov's dramas at the Art Theatre was to be its own eulogy to the poet: Chekhov's first drama, *Ivanov* was not yet in the repertoire, but the Art Theatre began the first season after Chekhov's death with *Ivanov*.

The Theatre which had already produced *Seagull* and *Uncle Vanya* did not find *Ivanov* a difficult challenge. The production proceeded with confidence and calm, following a familiar, well-worn path: there was no search required since the Theatre had already found everything. The tense atmosphere and mood of all other Art Theatre premieres – whether previous or current – was completely lacking at the opening of *Ivanov*. Instead the mood was that of collective sympathy. Chekhov's audience came to this Chekhov production full of the sadness of grief; they responded only with attentive and instantaneous sympathy to every mournful word of this much-loved writer, especially dear after such a permanent separation.

As far as I can remember, this Chekhov production did not receive a unanimous critical response. The reason for their disagreement – or source of the argument – was Mr Kachalov's performance: he transformed Ivanov's Hamletism into a kind of neurasthenia, playing him with an exhaustion which debased Chekhov's character. Earlier I quoted [page 6] the author's own opinion of his character – he had 'not lied by one centimetre, or exaggerated by one iota' about this feature or characteristic of our life. Likewise, the actor must 'not lie or be too clever by half' in the portrayal of the author's character.

There were aspects of exhaustion in Chekhov's Ivanov which the character himself constantly and deliberately articulates, and there are also elements of morbidity which, if you like, could be seen as neurasthenia or nervous debility. But this was only one symptom of the fact that Ivanov 'had taken a burden on his own shoulders, and his back then snapped'. There was no question that at 20 he 'was a hero who undertook every challenge and could do anything'; and it was accepted that until recently 'he had faith, and saw things differently from other people'. Even at the end, at the very edge of death, he was still head and shoulders above other people, and still one of the spiritual-elect although brought down by our whole way of life. For that reason this Ivanov expresses a real, vital and tragic characteristic of Russian reality.[5] This role was therefore understood, and when performed with delicacy, subtlety and sincerity, it was moving.

Another beautiful character in the play was Mr Stanislavski's Shabelsky, a pitiful figure who at times moved one to tears. Mrs Knipper's performance as Sarah [Anna] had much less artistic value, while there was even less value in the interpretation of Sashenka [Sasha] by Mrs Tarina, although drawn expressively and interestingly. However, Chekhov himself was not altogether happy with the way he created this female character – Sashenka is rather awkwardly placed and at a disadvantage in the play: she is there only to throw light on aspects of Ivanov, and is not interesting in her own right. Such a part can never work, so a Sashenka who entertains an audience would always help to make a successful performance. Mr Moskvin's performance as the narrow-minded but honest Lvov provided a rounded characterization. The secondary characters in the play were also successful, and offered no problematical challenge to the performers.

This was the way Chekhov's dramas were produced by the Art Theatre.

When he scarcely knew the Art Theatre, Chekhov wrote: 'This is the only Theatre which I love.' This love which Chekhov devoted to it on credit, so to speak, was justified by the Art Theatre for the rest of Chekhov's life. Everything that the stage can do for a dramatist was done for Chekhov. But Chekhov was no debtor: he brought the attention of Russia to this Theatre, and more than anyone else he helped it to rise to the heights at which the Art Theatre now stands. Without thinking about himself, he did even more. With his dramatic art he provided a challenge to the Art Theatre which required a new methodology, and even new principles of artistic staging. This stage gave life to a playwright who had previously seemed impossible to perform in the theatre, while the dramatist took the stage down a path which had seemed unobtainable. Theirs was a happy union.

No longer will anybody ever think of Chekhov as separate from the Art Theatre – or of the Art Theatre without Chekhov.

N. Efros

30 K.S. Stanislavski.

Pencil drawing by the artist A.A. Koiranski.

'SEAGULL'

This was put on for the first time on 17 December 1898. The parts were played as follows: Arkadina – O.L. Knipper; Trepliov – V.E. Meyerhold; Nina Zarechnaya – M.L. Roksanova; Trigorin – K.S. Stanislavski; Sorin – V.V. Luzhski; Dorn – A.L. Vishnevski; Masha – M.P. Lilina; Shamraev – A.R. Artem; [Polina] Shamraeva – E.M. Raevskaia; Medvedenko – I.A. Tikhomirov; the housemaid – M.P. Nikolaeva, the chef – B.M. Snigirev. The scenic design, as in all of Chekhov's plays, was by V.A. Simov.

After the first performance the play was taken off for about two weeks due to Mrs Knipper's illness, and then it played to full houses until the end of the season. At this time A.P. Chekhov was in Yalta. When they telegraphed him and wrote to him to tell him about the play's success, it took a long time before he believed it: he thought that they were hiding the truth from him out of friendship. He only came to Moscow in the spring but the Theatre was not open then.

With his arrival, close friendships quickly sprang up between Chekhov and the artists. The discussion was about a production of *Uncle Vanya* but Chekhov had retained friendly relations with many of the artists of the Imperial Maly Theatre and did not want to break the promise he had made earlier concerning their production of the play. Lenski, Yuzhin and the director, Kondratov, were pressing hard for a production of *Uncle Vanya* at the Maly Theatre. That spring, just at that time, there was a session of the Theatrical Literary Committee[60] and *Uncle Vanya* was not approved for performance or – to be more exact – it was approved 'on condition that the Third Act be re-written'. Chekhov, of course, did not agree to this rewrite, and gave the play to the Art Theatre.[61] The famous group photograph of Chekhov with the artists and directors of *Seagull* relates to this time[62] [see Page 21, Illustration 32]. In the following season *Seagull* was retained in the repertoire, but performed haphazardly, with long breaks. Kachalov still played Trigorin; Sorin was played by A.I. Zagarov, and Shamraev by B.M. Snigirev, etc.[sic]. *Seagull* was then taken out of the repertoire in 1902 and only reinstated in 1905, but without much success for the Art Theatre. The external trappings of the production [décor, *mise-en-scène*] were retained but the excitement which greeted the premiere did not recur and the performance was somewhat stale. For the revival at this time [1905] the part of Trepliov was shared by V.V. Maximov and Meyerhold; Nina Zarechnaya shared by Lilina and L.A. Kosminskaya; Masha by M.G. Savitskaya; Medvedenko by M.L. Los and N.A. Podgorni, while the other parts remained as before. The 1905–06 season was interrupted by the armed uprising in Moscow.[63] The Art Theatre went abroad and since then the *Seagull* has not been reinstated.[64]

Seagull [colour]

31 Sketch of the setting for Act I. V. Simov.

32 First read-through of *Seagull*.
Standing (from left to right): Nemirovich-Danchenko, Luzhski, Andreev, Grigorieva.
(Seated): Raevskaia, Vishnevski, Artem, Knipper, Stanislavski, Chekhov, Lilina, Roksanova, Meyerhold and Tikhomirov.

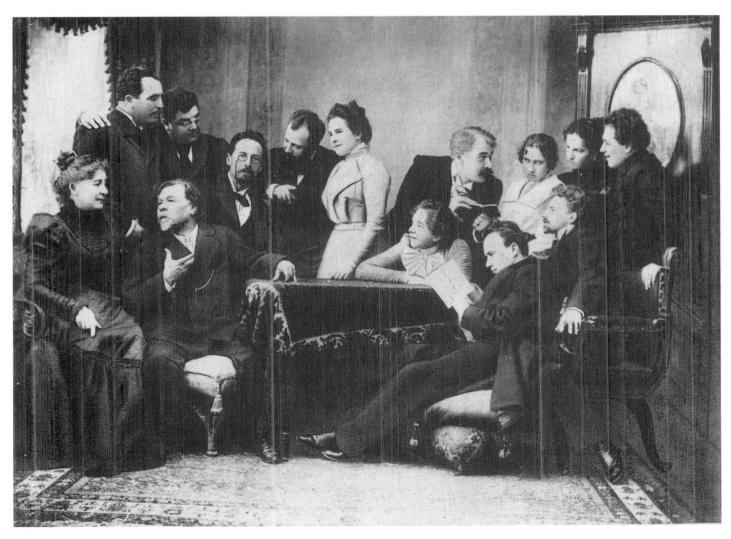

33 Exchanging impressions after the reading of *Seagull*.

34 Trepliov (Meyerhold): 'We shall open the curtain at exactly half past eight when the moon rises . . .'

35 Arkadina (Knipper): 'Ten or fifteen years ago there was music and singing by this lake, almost every day . . .'

SEAGULL Act II

36 Nina Zarechnaya (Roksanova): 'This seagull is a symbol too, I suppose . . .' (Photos by Scherer and Nabholtz).

37 Arkadina (Knipper): 'Tell me what is wrong with my son? Why is he so bored and depressed . . .?'

Act III

38 Sorin (Luzhski): 'Everything seems nasty to me . . .'

39 Arkadna (Knipper): 'You won't do anything like this again . . .'

40 Trigorin (Stanislavski): 'We're leaving, are we? More railway carriages, stations, buffets, chops and talk . . .'

41 Arkadina (Knipper): 'Here, a rouble for you all . . .'
(Photos by Scherer and Nabholtz.)

42 Dorn (Vishnevski): 'Tell me, where is Zarechnaya [Nina] these days? Where is she and how is she?'

43 Trigorin (Stanislavski): 'Irina Nikolaievna [Arkadina] said that you have forgotten the past and are no longer angry . . .'

44 Trigorin (Stanislavski): 'If I lived in a house by a lake like this, would I be writing [all the time] . . .?'
(Photos by Scherer and Nabholtz.)

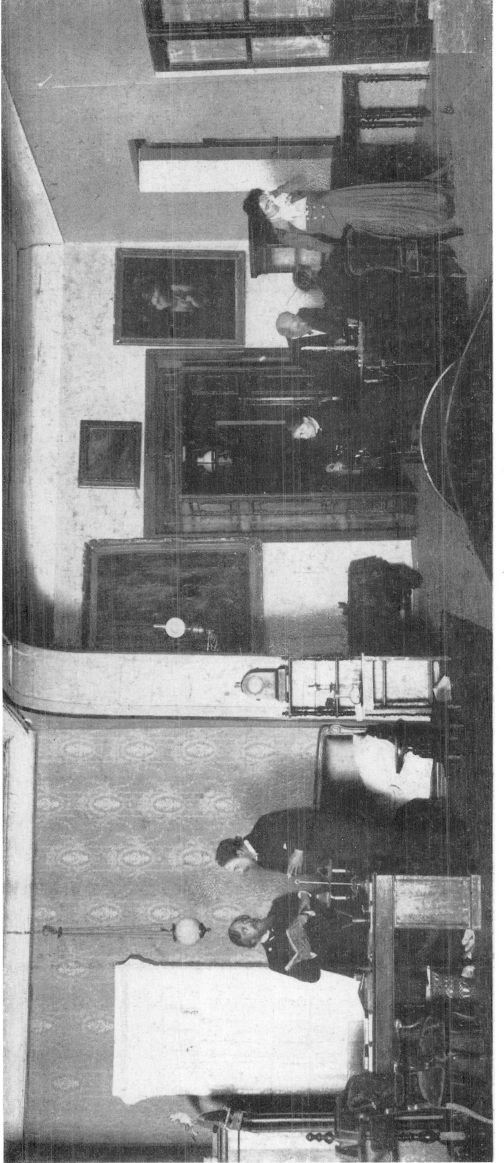

45 Dorn (*Vishnevski*): 'Get Irina Nikolaievna out of here, somehow. The fact is, Konstantin Gavrilovich has shot himself . . .'
(Photo by Scherer and Nabholtz.)

46 A.R. Artem (last portrait).
(Photo by Fisher.)

'UNCLE VANYA'

This was put on for the first time on 26 October 1899. The parts were played as follows: Elena – O.L. Knipper; Sonia – M.P. Lilina and V.A. Petrova; Astrov – K.S. Stanislavski; Voinitski [Vanya] – A.L. Vishnevski; Serebriakov – V.V. Luzhski; Voinitskaya [Mrs Voinitski] – E.M. Raevskaia; Telegin [Waffles] – A.R. Artem; Marina – M.A. Samarova [and A. Pomialova]; Labourer – N.G. Alexandrov [and N. Rumiantsev].

In the history of the Art Theatre there were very few examples of an immediate, incisive and complete success from the very first performance. With the exception of *Dr Stockman* [Ibsen's *Enemy of the People*] and *Lower Depths* [Gorki's *Na dne*], it may positively be said that such a success only happened with those plays where a significant role was given to crowd-scenes: *Tsar Fiodor Ivanovich*, *Julius Caesar* or *Brand* [Ibsen].[65] It was only long after the event that other so-called 'winners' were described as such. After the first performance of *Uncle Vanya* the feelings of the Theatre company, of the performers, was ambiguous and dissatisfied. With two or three exceptions, the newspaper reviews were also rather nebulous. After about ten performances of full houses, audience figures began to fall off quite quickly, and there were several performances when the house was only half full. *Uncle Vanya* was to become a mainstay of the Theatre's repertoire, one of its oldest workhorses, but only in later seasons.

The performers remained virtually unchanged except for a few cases of substitution caused by sudden illness. Until recently, the play has been performed 155 times.

The first discussions about the play took place with Chekhov himself participating. With his permission, the text was rewritten in places – particularly the monologues, which were strange to actors of the new order. Chekhov did not see *Uncle Vanya* in Moscow's first season, so when they began to persuade him to write a new play, he stubbornly refused and argued that he could not start a new work for the Theatre since he had not yet seen his plays in performance. That was why the Theatre decided to go to Yalta – this journey, with all the sets, costumes, lighting and the theatre workers, was a novelty in Russia.

In order to recoup the expense of the trip, it was decided to give four performances in Sevastopol[66] and eight in Yalta; and in order to increase box office returns, in addition to *Seagull* and *Uncle Vanya*, they also performed Hauptmann's *Lonely Lives* and Ibsen's *Hedda Gabler*.

Given the small theatres [and thus audience capacity] in Sevastopol and Yalta, they raised the seat prices to more than 1,000 roubles.

This spring trip to the South, with a youthful company, gave the Theatre [ensemble] a great deal of pleasure, particularly since it exceeded all expectations.

Chekhov's popularity in the Crimea was already considerable, but was further increased by the journey of the whole Theatre to perform his own plays for their favourite writer.

The reminiscences of this journey are bathed with Southern sunlight. Chekhov came to Sevastopol from Yalta, and the whole troupe met him at the docks. And after four performances in Sevastopol, they moved to Yalta where Chekhov's house – built by him and with the garden he had planted himself – was filled with the actors all day, enjoying the hospitality of the poet to whom they had become close over these two years.

Gorki was also in Yalta at the same time, and he had only just reached the height of his fame.[67] Imagine: spring; the sea; the sunlight; the close proximity of two of the most promising young writers; the young Theatre's success, celebrating not so much its achieved victory as its ardent hope for future success – and you will easily understand the joyous atmosphere experienced by the convivial Art Theatre family.

UNCLE VANYA

47 Sketch of setting for Act I. V. Simov.

48 [Left to right] Uncle Vanya (Vishnevski), Sonia (Lilina), Serebriakov (Luzhski), Waffles [Telegin] (Artem), Elena Andreievna (Knipper), Marina (Samarova), Astrov (Stanislavski) [Seated].

49 Telegin [Waffles] (Artem): 'Anyone who betrays a wife or a husband, could easily be untrustworthy enough to betray his country as well.'

50 Maria Vasilievna [Mrs Voinitski] (Raevskaia):
'I had a letter from Pavel Alekseyevich . . . He sent his new
pamphlet . . .'

51 Uncle Vanya (Vishnevski): 'Let me speak of my love. Just don't push me away . . .'

53 Labourer (N. Rumiantsev).

52 Uncle Vanya (Vishnevski) and Telegin (Artem).

54 Marina (Samarova).

55 Telegin (Artem), Maria Vasilievna [Mrs Voinitski] (Raevskaia), Uncle Vanya (Vishnevski).

56 Telegin (Artem).

57 *Uncle Vanya* – Sonia (Lilina).

58 *Uncle Vanya* – Professor Serebriakov (Luzhski).

33

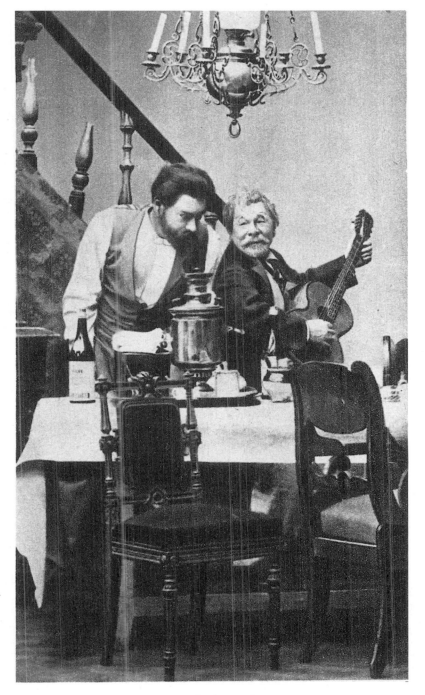

59 Astrov (K.S. Stanislavski), Waffles (A.R. Artem).
(Photo Scherer and Nabholtz.)

60 Marina (A. Pomialova) [to Serebriakov]: 'What is it, old chap? In pain? My own legs hurt, hurt so much . . .'

61 Uncle Vanya (Vishnevski).

62 Marina (A. Pomialova).

63 Telegin (Artem): 'My dear chap, I'm only too glad to oblige, but you know – people in the house are trying to sleep!'

64 Sonia (Lilina) and Marina (Samarova) [change of casting of Marina here].

65 Uncle Vanya (Vishnevski).

66 Uncle Vanya: 'Where is he? Ah, there he s!' (Fires at Serebriakov.) 'Bang!' [This action follows the action illustrated on page 37.]

67 A.R. Artem (Ilya Ilyich Telegin . . . *Uncle Vanya*).

68 Elena Andreievna (Knipper): 'Let me go! Leave me alone . . .'

69 Professor [Serebriakov] (Luzhski): 'We aren't made for living in the country . . .'

70 Uncle Vanya (Vishnevski): 'You write about art,
but you understand nothing about art . . .'
(Photos by Scherer and Nabholtz.)

71 Professor (Luzhski): 'I gladly accept your apologies and beg you to accept mine.'

72 Astrov (Stanislavski): 'How quiet. Pens scratching, crickets chirping. How warm, cosy. I don't want to leave now . . .'

73 Sonia (Lilina): 'We shall rest! We will hear angels, we will see the sky sparkle with diamonds . . .'
(Photos by Scherer and Nabholtz.)

74 Astrov (K.S. Stanislavski).
(Photo by Scherer and Nabholtz.)

'THREE SISTERS'

This was put on for the first time on 31 January 1901. The parts were played as follows: Olga – M.G. Savitskaia; Masha – O.L. Knipper; Irina – M.F. Andreeva; Andrei – V.V. Luzhski; Vershinin – K.S. Stanislavski; Tuzenbakh – V.E. Meyerhold; Solioni – M.A. Gromov (and afterwards by L.M. Leonidov); Kulygin – A.L. Vishnevski; Chebutykin – A.R. Artem; Natasha – M.P. Lilina; Rode – I.F. Moskvin; Fedotik – I.A. Tikhomirov; Ferapont – V.F. Gribunin; Anfisa – M.A. Samarova.[68]
Information for the publication of this album: this play has been performed 169 times.

Chekhov wrote *Three Sisters* in summer in Yalta, and then rewrote it in early autumn in Moscow. He spent two to three days on each act, but there were significant breaks between the acts. A sketch of the play in the form of short dialogues remained at his house [in Yalta].

With complete sincerity he said that he had written a vaudeville, and was taken aback at our amusement of this definition of *Three Sisters*.[69]

Chekhov was present for the first read-through of the play by the actors. As on another occasion when the actors plied him with questions about particular aspects of their parts which seemed unclear to them, Chekhov not only refused any lengthy explanations, but rather categorically answered them with short and monosyllabic words. For example, he was asked about the following:

Masha asks: 'Ti tum ti tum…?'
Vershinin replies: 'Ti tum ti tum…'
Masha asks: 'Tra-ra-ram, tum – tum?'
Vershinin replies: 'Tra-ra-ram, tum – tum.'

Shrugging his shoulders, Chekhov answered only with: 'Oh, nothing special. Just a joke.' And later on, however much they pestered him for an explanation of the joke, he simply did not answer. When the play was being rehearsed, Chekhov went off to Nice. And when the day of the premiere drew close, he went off to Naples, almost deliberately concealing his address.

However much he tried to hide his feelings, we felt them. He had written no plays for five years, and perhaps this time as well, the ghost of the first production of *Seagull* still frightened him.[70] The telegrams about its success must, however, have reassured and consoled him.

Given its ensemble playing, the friendliness of the performance, and maturity of form, *Three Sisters* was always seen in the theatre as the best of the Chekhov productions.

And when the Art Theatre went to St Petersburg with *Three Sisters* at the end of this season, it repeated the success of *Uncle Vanya*.

The parts in *Three Sisters* often went to other actors, so by the 150th performance, only O.L. Knipper and A.L. Vishnevski still played their original roles. Olga was played by N.S. Butova and M.N. Germanova on the death of Savitskaia; Irina went from M.F. Andreeva to M.N. Litovtsieva and then to V. V. Baranovskaia. Andrei was also played by A.I. Adashev; Vershinin by V.I. Kachalov, E.A. Lepkovski and L.M. Leonidov. Tuzenbakh finally went to V.I. Kachalov, and so on.

The period of *Three Sisters* plays a particularly important part in the personal relations between Chekhov and the Art Theatre. The friendly relations between the poet and the artists became stronger at this time, and this was also the time of Chekhov's marriage to O.L. Knipper.

THREE SISTERS [colour]

75 Sketch of the setting for Act IV. V. Simov.

THREE SISTERS Act I

76 Irina (Baranovskaia): 'I don't know why, but for some reason I feel so light-hearted . . .'

[Olga – next to Irina at the window, on the left of the illustration. Masha – reading a book, dressed in black.]

77 Olga (Butova).

78 Anfisa (Raevskaia): 'This is from the town council, from Mikhail Ivanych Protopopov . . . A cake . . .'

79 Tuzenbakh (V.I. Kachalov): 'Lieutenant-Colonel Vershinin . . .' [Introducing him.]

80 Olga (Butova): 'This is my brother, Andrei Sergeevich . . .'

81 Vershinin (Stanislavski): 'I often wonder what would happen if we could start our lives again, knowing what we know now . . .'

32 Solioni (Massalitinov): 'Tut, tut, tut! . . .'

83 Kulygin (A.L. Vishnevski): 'In this book, you will find the history of our school over the last fifty years . . .'
(Photos by Fisher.)

84 Masha (*Three Sisters*) O.L. Knipper.

(Photo by Fisher.)

85 Irina (Baranovskaia): 'Nikolai Lvovich, please don't talk to me of love.' [To Tuzenbakh.]

86 Natasha (Lilina): 'I'm late . . .'

87 Natasha (Lilina): 'Good day, Baron . . .'

88 Anfisa (Raevskaia).

89 Fedotik (Podgorni): 'Just a minute! . . .' [Taking photographs.] 'One! . . .'

90 Andrei (Luzhski): 'My dear, innocent darling, be my wife . . .' [To Natasha outside window.]
(Photos by Fisher.)

45

91 Fedotik (Podgorni), Rodé (Berensev), Irina (Baranovskaia) are singing 'Those mad nights'.
Vershinin (Stanislavski): 'Still, it's a shame that we're not young any more . . .'

92 Vershinin (Stanislavski): 'We aren't happy, we never are. We only desire it . . .'

93 Masha (Knipper): 'The Baron's drunk, the Baron's drunk!' [In the script, Masha is waltzing on her own.]

94 Andrei (Luzhski): 'There's a new entrance-hall, made of maple . . .'

95 Kulygin (Vishnevski): 'Yes, I also got tired at the meeting . . .'

96 Natasha (Lilina).

97 Natasha (Lilina): 'I'll be home in half an hour . . .'
(Photos by Fisher.)

98 Olga (*Three Sisters*) N.S. Butova.

99 Vershinin (*Three Sisters*) K.S. Stanislavski
(Photo by Fisher.)

100 Kulygin (*Three Sisters*) A.L. Vishnevski.

101 Olga (Butova): 'You were so rude to Nanny just now . . .' [To Natasha.]

102 Vershinin (Stanislavski), Kulygin (Vishnevski), Irina (Babanovskaia), Tuzenbakh (Kachalov), Masha (Knipper).

103 Fedotik (Podgorni): 'The fire took everything from me, everything! Everything I had . . .'

104 Masha (Knipper).

105 Olga (Butova): 'Don't cry, my child, don't cry . . . I'm suffering . . .'

106 Vershinin (Stanislavski): [Singing.]: 'As everyone has always found, / It's love that makes the world go round.' Masha (Knipper) [Singing.]: Ti tum ti tum . . .'

107 Fedotik (Podgorni): 'Stand still . . . One last time . . .'

108 Masha (Knipper): 'There he sits, as usual . . .'

109 Kulygin (Vishnevski): You're incorrigible, Ivan Romanich. Incorrigible.'
[To Chebutykin.]

110 Irina (Baranovskaia): 'What happened outside the theatre yesterday?' Tuzenbakh (Kachalov): 'I shall be back with you again in an hour . . .' (Photos by Fisher.)

111 Irina (V.V. Baranovskaia).

112 Ferapont (V.F. Gribunin), Andrei (V.V. Luzhski).
(Photos by Fisher.)

113 Tuzenbakh – *Three Sisters* – Kachalov.

114 Solioni (Massalitinov): 'He hardly had time to sigh when a bearskin fell on him . . .' [Quoting, before the duel.]

115 Natasha (Lilina) [Through the window.]: 'Who's talking so loudly . . .?'

116 Olga (Butova): Nanny, give those musicians something! . . .'

117 Vershinin (Stanislavski): 'I came to say goodbye . . .'

118 Kulygin (Vishnevski): 'Do I look like a [the] German teacher?' [At his school.]

119 Olga (Butova): 'The music is so cheerful, so happy. And it seems that before long we too shall find out why we are living, why we are suffering. If only we knew! If only we knew! . . .' [Curtain.]
(Photos by Fisher.)

120 Vershinin (Stanislavski).

121 Anfisa (Samarova).

122 Ferapont (Gribunin).

123 Solioni (Leonidov).

124 Kulygin (Vishnevski), Irina (Baranovskaia).

125 Rodé (Moskvin).

126 Irina (Baranovskaia).

127 Chebutykin (Artem).

128 Andrei (Luzhski), Ferapont (Gribunin).
(Photos by Fisher.)

53

'CHERRY ORCHARD'

Chekhov's swan song.

'I can only write about four lines a day, and those with unbearable difficulties.'

This is from a letter by Chekhov in the autumn of 1903.

The Theatre particularly needed his play for this season. It had been decided to put on only *Julius Caesar* and Chekhov's new play. On this occasion he was dutifully meeting certain needs of the Theatre, and would have been only too delighted had they told him he could put the play off for a year. When he completed the play, he was not completely sure that it had come out the way he wanted.

He adamantly decided to spend this winter in Moscow, and the doctors allowed him to move to Moscow only when the dry frosts had set in. Before he arrived, he enquired anxiously how the Theatre had received the play, and how the parts would be cast.

By this time he was so intimately involved with the Art Theatre that he concerned himself with all the details of its life and work;[71] he was a shareholder of the Theatre; he also requested that they send him all the plays which were presented in the Theatre since he was prepared to read and comment on them.

Perhaps it is not necessary to add that the Art Theatre established strong and friendly relations with his family – with his mother, his brother, Ivan Pavlovich, and in particular with his sister, Maria Pavlovna who, with such love and energy, consecrated her life and work to his papers – the collections of letters and literary and dramatic materials – and after his death, acted as the guardian of his dear memory.

Chekhov stayed in Moscow from the beginning of November. At first he attended the rehearsals of *Cherry Orchard* but because he was not used to the actors' slow development and identification with their characters, he became very uneasy and stopped going to rehearsals.[72]

He did not believe it would be successful.

Half-joking, half-serious, he would say: 'Buy it for 3,000 [roubles].' And we answered him by saying: 'Do you want us to guarantee 10,000?' As usual, he did not like being involved in arguments. Full of lack of confidence, he just silently shook his head.

The premiere took place on 17 January 1904, and completely by chance it coincided with Chekhov's name day.

With the premonition that they would never again have a better occasion to express their feelings, the author's fervent and enthusiastic fans used the day of the premiere to arrange a huge celebratory event. After Act III, speeches were read, and [laurel] wreaths were brought to him from all of Moscow's literary and artistic circles.

It was one of the most unforgettable of the Art Theatre's performances. The parts were played as follows: Ranevskaya – O.L. Knipper; Gayev – K.S. Stanislavski; Anya – M.P. Lilina; Varya – M.F. Andreeva; Lopakhin – L.M. Leonidov; Trofimov – V.I. Kachalov; Simeonov-Pishchik – V.F. Gribunin; Firs – A.R. Artem; Charlotta – E.P. Muratova; Yasha – N.G. Alexandrov; Dunyasha – S.V. Khaliutina. Later Gayev was understudied by V.V. Luzhski; Anya was gradually taken over by L.A. Kosminskaia; by M.A. Zhdanova and R.M. Koreneva; turn and then turn about Varya was played by M.G. Savitskaia, and after her death by M.P. Lilina. Lopakhin was played by N.O. Massalitinov; Trofimov by Podgorni, Dunyasha by L.I. Dimitrevskaia, and so on.

However, the play only reached out to a larger public in the following season. In this first season, Chekhov's subtle, delicate writing, his realism which was pared away to symbolism,[73] and the beauty of feelings, were not at all appreciated.

Up to the present, the play has been performed more than 200 times.

129 A.R. Artem (Firs). (*Cherry Orchard*.)

131 Lopakhin
(Massalitinov).

132 Liubov Andreievna [Ranevskaya] (Knipper):
'The nursery, my dear, is a lovely room . . .'

130 Yepikhodov (Moskvin).

133 Liubov Andreievna [Ranevskaya] (Knipper): 'If there is one thing that's
interesting in the whole province, it's our cherry orchard . . .' [To Lopakhin.]

134 Lopakhin (Massalitinov): 'Your brother, Leonid Andreevich [Gayev], calls
me a lout and a money-grubbing peasant . . .'

135 Gayev (Stanislavski): 'Dear, much respected bookcase! I salute your existence . . .'
(Photos by Fisher.)

136 Lopakhin (Massalitinov).

137 Gayev (Stanislavski): 'That's our famous Jewish band . . .'

138 Gayev (Stanislavski) [To Yasha.]: 'What is it? Why are you always hovering around in front of me? . . .'

139 Gayev (Stanislavski): 'You can take this road . . .' [To the passer-by.]

140 Trofimov (Podgorni): 'The vast majority of the intelligentsia that I know, seek after nothing, do nothing, and are as yet incapable of hard work . . .'

141 [Boris] Simeonov-Pishchik (*Cherry Orchard*) – Gribunin.

142 Lopakhin (Massalitinov): 'Let me ask you, how can [I make] you understand me? . . .' [Referring to the forthcoming auction.]

CHERRY ORCHARD Act II

143 Trofimov (Podgorni): 'Happiness is coming, Anya, I feel it. I already see it . . .'.
(Photo by Fisher.)

144 Liubov Andreievna [Ranevskaya] (Knipper): 'You look so funny . . .!'

145 Guests: 'Bravo, Charlotta Ivanovna! . . .'

146 Charlotta (Muratova): 'Ein, zwei, drei . . .'

147 Simeonov-Pishchik (Gribunin): 'Imagine, most charming Charlotta Ivanovna, I'm simply in love with you!' (Photos by Fisher.)

148 Lopakhin (*Cherry Orchard*) L.M. Leonidov.

CHERRY ORCHARD Act III

149 Cotillion. [This dance is rarely performed, usually only waltz music is used, as specified in the original.]

63

150 Yasha (Alexandrov): 'Yepikhodov's broken a billiard cue . . .' [Trying to restrain his laughter.]

151 Lopakhin (Massalitinov): 'I bought it! . . .' [The cherry orchard at the auction.]

152 The Post
Office Clerk
(Tezavrovski).

153 Lopakhin (Massalitinov): 'Oh, why, oh why
didn't you listen to me? . . .' [To Ranevskaya.]

154 Anya (Zhdanova): 'We'll plant
a new orchard, more glorious than
this one . . .' [To Ranevskaya.]
(Photos by Fisher.)

155 Gayev (*Cherry Orchard*). K.S. Stanislavski.

156 Artist of the Moscow Art Theatre, V.I. Kachalov.

Pencil drawing by the artist A.A. Koiranski.

157 Lopakhin (Massalitinov): 'Ladies and gentlemen, don't forget the train leaves in only 46 minutes . . .' [In the original script, it is 47 minutes.]

158 Lopakhin (Massalitinov): 'Drink it up, Yasha, anyway . . .' [Referring to the champagne he had bought.]

159 Varya (Lilina): 'Yes, life has gone from this house. And it will never come back . . .' [To Lopakhin.]

160 Lopakhin (Massalitinov).

161 Charlotta (Muratova): 'I haven't anywhere to live in town . . .'
(Photos by Fisher.)

67

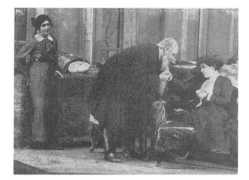

162 Simeonov-Pishchik (Gribunin): 'Everything in this world comes to an end . . .'

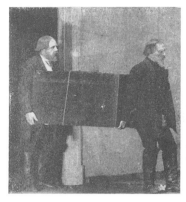

163 Their things are carried out.

164 Liubov Andreievna [Ranevskaya] (Knipper): 'I'm leaving with two things still on my mind . . .' [To Lopakhin.]

165 Anya (Lilina): 'Goodbye, house! Goodbye, old life! . . .'

166 Liubov Andreievna [Ranevskaya] (Knipper): 'My life, my youth, my happiness, goodbye! . . .' Gayev (Stanislavski): 'My sister! My sister! . . .'

167 Firs (Pavlov): 'They've gone. . . . They forgot me . . .' (Photos by Fisher.)

168 Dunyasha (Khalitina), Post Office Clerk
(Cezavrovski).

169 Charlotta (Muratova).

170 Yepikhodov (Moskvin).

171 Anya (Zhdanova),
Trofimov (Podgorni).

172 Firs (Artem). [See p.68 for different casting.]

173 Charlotta (Muratova),
Lopakhin (Leonidov).

174 Passer-by (Baliev).
(Photos by Fisher.)

176 Charlotta (Muratova), Dunyasha (Khaliutina), Yasha (Alexandrov),
Yepikhodov (Moskvin).

175 Liubov Andreievna Ranevskaya
(O.L. Knipper).

177 Gayev (Stanislavski), Anya (Lilina).

178 Trofimov (Kachalov), Anya (Lilina).

179 Yasha (Alexandrov).

180 Varya (Lilina), Anya (Zhdanova), Gayev (Stanislavski).
[Casting changes of Varya and Anya.]

181 Stationmaster (Gorich).
(Photos by Fisher.)

182 Artist of the Moscow Art Theatre, L.M. Leonidov.

Pencil drawing by the artist A.A. Koiranski.

'IVANOV' AND THE MINIATURES

Ivanov was put on for the first time on 19 October 1904. The parts were played as follows: Ivanov – V.I. Kachalov; Sarah – O.L. Knipper; Lebedev – V.V. Luzhski; Ziuziushka [Zinaida, Lebedev's wife][74] – M.A. Samarova; Sasha – L.U. Tarina; Shabelsky – K.S. Stanislavski; Borkin – L.M. Leonidov; Babakina – N.S. Butova; Kosykh – V.F. Gribunin; Lvov – I.M. Moskvin; in other roles, E.P. Muratova, and others.

After Chekhov's death, the Art Theatre had to put on his fifth great play, *Ivanov*. This is the only Chekhov play which was immediately successful, from the premiere onwards; that was because there were clear elements of the 'old theatre' which ensured the play's success, and also because the innovatory aspect (the first act) involved methods which the Theatre had already developed – ready-made elements that had already been tried out and which therefore also ensured a high level of performance.

In Chekhov's creative output – in the vast majority of his short stories – one could always feel theatrical elements. This was not the theatricality of the 'old-style' theatre, but an innovatory theatricality which gave the material new characteristics, whether in the theatre or in literature. The closer the theatre came to Chekhov's creative output, the more he began to feel the possibility of staging his short stories. This eventually motivated Stanislavski into devising a plan: staging a special genre of small dramatic works under the general heading of 'miniatures'.[75]

No doubt the public at large realized that the idea of such productions was created in the Art Theatre, and was then widely developed throughout Russia.

The Art Theatre tried an experiment: they staged six to seven of Chekhov's short stories, most of which were then postponed after the dress rehearsal, but three of them were given public performances. These were *Surgery* [*Khirurgiia*] (with I.M. Moskvin and V.F. Gribunin); *The Conspirator* [*Zloumyshlennik*] (with M.A. Gromov, A.L. Vishnevski and others), and *Sergeant Prishibeev* [*Unter Prishibeev*] (with V.V. Luzhski and others).[76]

IVANOV [colour]

183 Sketch of setting for Act I. V. Simov.
[In the original, this preceded *Seagull* on p.41.]

184 Anna Petrovna Ivanova (Knipper), Shabelski (Stanislavski).

Act II

185 Babakina (Butova): 'Lottery tickets, my dear Zinaida Savishna, are rising fast . . .'

186 (Leonidov): 'Noble Signorina, I make bold to congratulate the universe on the birth of such a wondrous blossom as you . . .'
[To Sasha.]

187 Shabelski (Stanislavski): 'I'm walking around in a velvet jacket and a valet dresses me: I'm a wretch and a serf-owner . . .'

188 Ivanov (Kachalov): 'I used to work hard and think hard, but never got tired . . .'

Act III

189 Shabelski (Stanislavski): 'Yesterday, at [Martha] Babakina's, there was a delicious snack. Boletus [white] mushrooms . . .'

190 Kosykh (Gribunin): 'I've been cleaned out! That Barabanov gambles like a professional . . .' [This is a literal translation of Efros' caption. In the original script, the implication is: 'That Barabanov's no good at cards . . .']

191 Lebedev (Luzhski): 'For you, a period of mourning and grief is at hand . . .'

192 Ivanov (Kachalov): 'I believed in different things from other people, married a different kind of woman, lost my head, took risks . . .'

193 Ivanov (Kachalov): 'A naïve man's a fool . . .' [To Sasha.]

194 Ivanov (Kachalov): 'Then you may as well know – you'll soon be dead . . .' [To Anna.]

Act IV

195 Lebedev (Luzhski): 'Well, now they're all howling . . .'

196 Ivanov (Kachalov): 'Leave me alone!' (Shoots himself.)

Printing by the 'Kopeika' Printing Company
St Petersburg, Ligovskaia, No. 24.

ENDNOTES

1 The use of upper case for 'Theatre' here specifically denotes the Moscow Art Theatre, a short-hand used throughout the original Introductions by Nemirovich-Danchenko and Nikolai Efros, as distinct from 'theatre' in general.

2 Nemirovich-Danchenko expresses the contemporary and subsequent views of Chekhov's 'melancholy' – a major source of disagreement between Chekhov and the Moscow Art Theatre. In addition to most of his one-act vaudevilles, most of the major plays were called comedies: only *Uncle Vanya* is subtitled 'Scenes from country life', while *Three Sisters* is called a 'drama'. All the others are subtitled 'comedies' although it was only near the end of the 20th century that the major plays were performed more humorously. The idea still persists of Chekhov's 'melancholy'.

3 Isaac Ilyich Levitan (1860–1900). See Illustration 14, Page 10. The painting has been described as: 'Hayricks in Moonlight'.

4 Andrei Prozorov's reference to Testov's Restaurant in Moscow, Act II, *Three Sisters*. Chekhov was in fact in Rome at the time of the final rehearsals, and before the premiere, having fled from Moscow in December 1990 out of irritation and depression. Nemirovich-Danchenko is of course writing generally about performances of *Three Sisters*. The first performance took place on 31 January 1901, the third time a Chekhov play was premiered in his absence. From Italy, Chekhov returned to Yalta, his Crimean 'exile', where the warmer climate was meant to improve his failing health.

5 This was the first public performance at the Aleksandrinski (*to use the most common English title – or Alexandra, Laurence Senelick's most accurate title, or Alexandrina, or Hingley's Alexandrine*) Theatre, St Petersburg, on 17 October 1896. For a detailed description of the production, the rehearsal and performance conditions, and disastrous reception, see L. Senelick, *The Chekhov Theatre*, Cambridge: CUP, 1997, pp.28–37. See also V. Gottlieb, *Chekhov in Performance in Russia and Soviet Russia*, Cambridge: Chadwyck-Healey, 1984, pp.15–16. See also R. Hingley, *The Oxford Chekhov*, London: Oxford University Press, Vol.1, *The Short Plays*, 1968; Vol. 2, *Platonov, Ivanov, The Seagull*, 1967; Vol. 3, *Uncle Vanya, Three Sisters, The Cherry Orchard, The Wood-Demon*, 1964. Hingley's Appendices to each volume give full production histories, and selections from Chekhov's letters on the plays. These translations of the plays are more accurate than any other existing English 'versions' or 'adaptations'. The great actress Vera Komissarzhevskaya played Nina.

6 Vladimir Ivanovich Nemirovich-Danchenko was a playwright as well as Stanislavski's co-founder of the Moscow Art Theatre. See Biographical Notes, and L. Senelick, *The Chekhov Theatre*, op. cit., and Nemirovich-Danchenko's autobiography, *My Life in the Russian Theatre*, London and USA: Geoffrey Bles, 1937 & 1968. See also R. Hingley, *A New Life of Chekhov*, London: Oxford University Press, 1976, pp.220–4.

7 Efros is exaggerating Stanislavski's views on Chekhov's plays – in fact, Stanislavski's view of *Seagull* was that: 'It seemed that it was not scenic, that it was monotonous and boresome' (sic). See Stanislavski's autobiography, *My Life in Art*, USA & London: Geoffrey Bles, first published 1924, p.321. Jean Benedetti's biography of Stanislavski and a forthcoming new biography by Anatoly Smeliansky for CUP will finally change the false perceptions of Stanislavski and his 'System'. Smeliansky, while previously Literary Manager (the post held originally by Nikolai Efros) and currently Director of the Moscow Art Theatre, is also a brilliant critic and theatre historian. See also R. Hingley, *A New Life of Chekhov*, op. cit., and various collections of Chekhov's letters.

8 Alexei Tolstoi's *Tsar Fiodor* is the second play in his trilogy beginning with *The Death of Ivan the Terrible* and ending with *Boris Godunov*. *Tsar Fiodor* was directed by Stanislavski and designed by Viktor Simov, and was the first production of the Moscow Art Theatre, performed at the Hermitage Theatre in October 1898, the same year as the MAT production of *Seagull*.

9 Efros mention of 'Devil's Island' is significant given Chekhov's very public support of Emile Zola and others over the Dreyfus Affair, a scandal which divided European opinion. A French Jew and Captain on the French General Staff, Alfred Dreyfus was set up with forged documents, and after a secret court martial, sent to the French penal colony on Devil's Island, Cayenne, in 1894, falsely accused of treason. The affair split opinion between the reactionary and anti-Semitic anti-'Dreyfusards' – and their progressive opponents, led by Emile Zola who himself was briefly imprisoned for his defence of Dreyfus. Chekhov's support immediately aligned him with Russian and European progressive opinion, and led to a major rift with his friend and publisher Alexei Suvorin, the owner of the right-wing newspaper *Novoie vremia (New Time)*. It is one of several political activities which clearly demonstrate that Chekhov was a democrat and progressive. The matter of penal servitude was particularly close to Chekhov given his eight-month journey in 1890 to the Russian penal island of Sakhalin to conduct a survey (and open a clinic), a journey which fatally damaged his health. His subsequent publication, *The Island of Sakhalin (or Sakhalin Island)* was published as a book (Chekhov's lengthiest work) by *Russkaya mysl* in 1895, and had

a major effect on his contemporaries, 'raising Sakhalin from obscurity, bringing the settlement and Siberian penal conditions in general, to public notice' (R. Hingley, *A New Life of Chekhov*, op. cit. p.144), and which, in turn led to some significant penal reform. Little known outside Russia, it was finally translated into English as: *The Island, A Journey to Sakhalin*, USA: Washington Square Press, 1967, then London: Century Hutchinson Ltd, 1987, with an introduction by Irina Ratushinshkaya.

10 This is one of several occasions in his introduction where Efros seems either contradictory or unclear. He is probably referring to the fact that Chekhov had not yet seen a performance as distinct from a rehearsal. There is also the point, reiterated throughout, that Chekhov loved the MAT without reservation, whereas it is well-known that he was constantly unhappy with Stanislavski's interpretation and production of his own plays – see Notes 2 and 30.

11 Writing as he was in 1914, Efros is amazingly prescient about the enduring qualities of what were, for that time, innovatory and even strangely 'plotless' new plays. It is worth remembering that this was before the outbreak of World War I; before the two revolutions in 1917, and the end of the Tsarist regime; before the Bolsheviks took power under Lenin; and before the resulting Civil War and foreign intervention. Both in Russia and abroad, Chekhov's plays come second only to Shakespeare in popularity and performance. See T. Shakh-Azizova, 'Chekhov on the Russian Stage', in V. Gottlieb & P. Allain, *The Cambridge Companion to Chekhov*, Cambridge: CUP, 2000, p.162. See also L. Senelick, *The Chekhov Theatre*, op. cit.

12 A.F. Koni – see Biographical Notes.

13 Efros is referring to the first four-act play which Chekhov wrote, probably in the early 1880s, and to which he gave no title. Like *Wood Demon* and *Ivanov*, he retained the then still current convention of scenic division each time a character entered on stage, an old-fashioned convention dropped with *Seagull*. Generally known as *Platonov*, it was neither published nor performed in his lifetime. The first performance was planned by Max Reinhardt in 1928 but dropped, and then adapted and directed by Helmut Ebbs for the Preussiches Theatre in Gera, Germany. See L. Senelick, *The Chekhov Theatre – Index of Chekhov Productions*, op. cit., under the heading 'Untitled', pp.420–1. The play's most exciting reincarnation was in the brilliant film, *An Unfinished Piece for Mechanical Piano* (1976) in a version directed by Nikita Mikhalkov, adapted with Alexander Adabashian, which, in turn, prompted Trevor Griffiths' version for Britain's RNT, *Piano*, in 1990. See E. Braun's excellent analysis, 'From *Platonov* to *Piano*' in *The Cambridge Companion to Chekhov*, op. cit., pp.43–56. It had earlier been adapted by Michael Frayn as *Wild Honey*, staged by the same National Theatre in 1984 to considerable popular acclaim, and explored by Braun in the above-mentioned chapter.

14 The play was, in fact, only acquired in 1920, by the Soviet Central State Literary Archive, and first published by them in 1923 as *An unpublished play of A.P. Chekhov*, edited by N.F. Belchikov. It was then published in the 1933 *Collected Works*, under the title *Fatherlessness (Bezotsovshchina)*, although there is some disagreement as to whether this is the same play as we now know as *Platonov*. See E. Braun, ibid., and R. Hingley, *The Oxford Chekhov*, op. cit., Vol. 2, 1967, *Platonov* and Appendix 1.

15 Efros supplies his own correction to this a few paragraphs later rendered, as in the original, in a footnote. In spite of the footnote, however, Efros still somewhat over-states the case given that the major failure was only with *Seagull*'s first production at the Imperial Alexandrinski Theatre. See Note 5. Productions of the one-act plays in particular, such as *The Bear*, produced at Korsh's private theatre, were well received. (For Korsh, see Biographical Notes.) As 'vaudevilles', however, it might be argued that they were seemingly more conventional, and Chekhov's sometimes 'subversion' of the genre to his own purpose went unnoticed. See T. Shakh-Azizova, *Chekhov on the Russian Stage* in V. Gottlieb & P, Allain, *The Cambridge Companion to Chekhov*, op. cit. Shakh-Azizova writes: 'The secret of their success was clearly evident: Chekhov introduced many changes to the conventional vaudeville: omitting the traditional couplets, adding "true-to-life" features, and ridiculing the traditional plots, often to the point of absurdity, while basically observing the rules of the genre' (p.162). See V. Gottlieb, *Chekhov and the Vaudeville*, CUP Cambridge, 1982. See Notes 68 and 71.

16 [Original footnote by Efros] It is only fair to remember that the Petersburg production of *Ivanov* at the Aleksandrinski Theatre was a great success. If we are not mistaken, it was put on at a benefit for the director [F.A. Fedorov-]Yurkovski. This production was described in an article by Gleb Uspenski – Editor [Efros].

17 Efros does not provide the full name of the broad-minded director-manager of the Alexandrinski Theatre. F.A. Fedorov-Yurkovski decided to stage *Ivanov* for his Benefit Night, an unusual choice given the Imperial Alexandrinski Theatre's usual repertoire. See L. Senelick, *The Chekhov Theatre*, op. cit., pp.19–24. To avoid confusion, I have used Senelick's transliteration here.

18 A similar character is to be found in Chekhov's short story of 1891, *V Moskve (In*

Moscow), a parody of Russian 'Hamletism' as originally exposed by Ivan Turgenev in his seminal essay *Hamlet and Don Quixote* (1850). Chekhov treats the 'Hamlet figure' in Russian literature in two inter-related ways. He often parodies those characters who see themselves as 'Hamlet but are really more like Tartuffe'. Thus the stereotypic 'Moscow Hamlet' constantly provides himself (the historical position of women means that this is invariably a male character) with a whole series of alibis for doing nothing positive or significant – or, simply, for doing *nothing*. Or Chekhov treats the stereotype by exposing the mental cost and disability as represented by the title-character in *Ivanov* where the attempt to meet the challenge of changing contemporary reality first saps then destroys the individual. In his Appendix to *Ivanov*, R. Hingley quotes Chekhov on the character: 'But at hardly 30 or 35 he's already tired and bored. He hasn't grown a decent moustache yet, but he's already laying down the law…', *The Oxford Chekhov*, op. cit., *Ivanov*, Appendix II, p.291. This relates also to Vanya in *Uncle Vanya*, to Andrei in *Three Sisters*, but centrally to Ivanov. The 'type' (which nonetheless always remains an individual in Chekhov's work) lives in a milieu clearly described by Viktor Simov, the MAT's designer of all Chekhov's plays, as one in which: 'colours fade, thoughts become debased, energy is smothered in a dressing-gown, ardour is stifled by a house-coat, talent dries up like a plant without water' (quoted in M.N. Pozharskaya, *Russkoe teatralno-dekoratsionnoe iskusstvo*, Moscow: 1970, p.124). This milieu is summed up by the Russian word 'poshlost' – 'untranslatable by any single word…it encompasses philistinism, the petty, the trivial, the mundane, and the banal: indicative of human behaviour and attitudes, it becomes a social disease and thus also a spiritual disease. . .', V. Gottlieb in *Chekhov and the Vaudeville*, op. cit. p.147. See Efros on *Ivanov*, p.17, and Note 55.

[19] According to R. Hingley's Appendix II to *Ivanov* in *The Oxford Chekhov*, op. cit., p.284, the first performance at Korsh's Theatre in Moscow took place on 19 November 1987. This is also borne out by Chekhov's letter to his brother Alexander, written from Moscow on 20 November 1887. For a full description of performance and response, see R. Hingley, *The Oxford Chekhov*, Vol. 2; Hingley's *A New Life of Chekhov*, and L. Senelick's *The Chekhov Theatre*, op. cit. Also Patrice Pavis, '*Ivanov*': *the invention of a negative dramaturgy* in *The Cambridge Companion to Chekhov*, op. cit., pp.70–9. And see various collections of letters available in English – such as those translated and edited by Avraham Yarmolinsky, New York: Viking Press Inc., 1973, and *Letters of Anton Chekhov*, translated by Michael Henry Heim in collaboration with Simon Karlinsky (selected, introduced and with commentary by Simon Karlinsky), New York: Harper & Row Publishers Inc., and London: Bodley Head, 1973. See Biographical Notes for note on Korsh. The actress's full name was A. Ya. Glama-Meshcherskaya.

[20] Part of the problem was that the tone of the production, and lack of interpretative understanding, made it unclear to the audience whether Chekhov was in fact approving of 'the Hamlet-figure' or parodying him.

[21] See Biographical Notes.

[22] See Senelick's *Index of Chekhov Productions*, op. cit. and Patrick Miles, ed., trans., *Chekhov on the British Stage*, Cambridge: CUP, 1993.

[23] See Biographical Notes.

[24] The word 'mood' – or in Russian, 'nastroenie' – has since become commonplace in relation to Chekhov's plays, and Efros's reiteration of the word is significant: it was exactly that feature which made the plays so innovatory and experimental, and, by the same token, so misunderstood. Only Turgenev in *A Month in the Country* had previously attempted anything approaching it in the theatre – but neither the theatre nor Turgenev himself took his dramatic works seriously, a dismissal which lasted much longer than the dismissal of Chekhov's plays. There was no equivalent to the Moscow Art Theatre in 1850 when Turgenev wrote the play.

[25] See Note 7.

[26] See E. Braun, *Stanislavsky and Chekhov* in *The Director and the Stage*, London: Methuen, 1982; L. Senelick's *The Chekhov Theatre*, op. cit.; V. Gottlieb, *Chekhov in Performance in Russia and Soviet Russia*, Cambridge: Chadwyck-Healey, 1984; A. Smeliansky, *Chekhov at the Moscow Art Theatre* in V. Gottlieb & P. Allain, eds, *The Cambridge Companion to Chekhov*, op. cit. See also Stanislavski, *My Life in Art*, op. cit. and Nemirovich-Danchenko, *My Life in The Russian Theatre*, op. cit. Full details in Note 7.

[27] Strangely, Efros omits Stanislavski's performance as Trigorin in *Seagull*. See also R. Hingley, *Seagull* in *The Oxford Chekhov*, Vol. 2, and Appendix III, London: Oxford University Press, 1967.

[28] *Russian Thought* or *Russkaya mysl*. Hingley translates it as *Russian Idea*.

[29] From October 1898 to December 1901, the first productions by the MAT took place at the Hermitage Theatre. From October 1902 they used the Kamergerski Theatre.

[30] It is significant, but common at the time that Efros always refers to all of Chekhov's plays as 'dramas', and never as 'comedies' – a view that virtually all interpreters of the plays held for many years subsequently. This was a major source of disagreement between Chekhov – and Stanislavski, and the MAT. This is particularly evident in relation to *Cherry Orchard* – see collected letters, such as those edited by Yarmolinsky and Karlinsky (Note 19), and L. Friedland, ed., *Chekhov – Letters on the short story, the drama and other literary topics*, London: Vision Press Ltd., 1965 (and USA: Benjamin Blom, Inc., 1964). See also Note 2 and Note 69.

[31] This, too, was a common view of Chekhov's plays, held by Stanislavski and others of Chekhov's contemporaries, and that loading the plays with detailed *naturalism* was

doing the plays a serious disservice. Only Nemirovich-Danchenko realized that there was more to the plays than 'realism' – although it took him until the 1930s to realize. As he put it: 'There is no denying that our theatre was at fault in failing to grasp the full meaning of Chekhov, his sensitive style and his extraordinarily delicate contours . . . *Chekhov refined his realism to the point where it became symbolic*, and it took a long time before we succeeded in conveying the subtle texture of his work. Maybe the theatre simply handled him too roughly.' – Quoted in M.N. Stroeva, *Rezhisserskie iskaniia Stanislavskogo, 1898–1917*, Moscow, 1973, p.121. Efros seems to have realized this earlier, see Note 73.

[32] Alexander Ostrovsky's play *Storm* (*Groza*, 1860), among others of his plays, illustrates Efros's point powerfully, but it could be argued that for that very reason Ostrovsky is not really 'conventional'. Earlier, Turgenev's very different *A Month in the Country* (*Mesiats v derevne*, 1850) illustrates 'mood' in a pre-Chekhovian way. 'Mood' is also evident in Pushkin's dramas, and in some of Tolstoi's plays, but not as the defining characteristic of the plays' tone. See Note 24.

[33] Literally, '*meiningenstvo*'. Efros refers to the Meiningen Theatre, established initially in 1831, but then shortly after his accession taken over by the Duke Georg of Saxe-Meiningen (1826–1914) as his own 'artistic director', with his wife, Ellen Franz (1839–1923), and the director Ludwig Chronegk (1837–91). The company's influence on European (and subsequently American) theatre was immense, and created a hitherto unknown realism in staging, unique historical accuracy, an emphasis on the actor in a designed context, an innovatory treatment of crowd scenes, and the depiction of movement. Their work, touring Europe, directly influenced, among others, André Antoine in Paris, Frank Benson and G.T. Grein in London, Otto Brahm in Berlin, and Stanislavski. See E. Braun, *The Meiningen Theatre*, *The Director and the Stage*, op. cit.

[34] See Note 8.

[35] Tolstoi's *The Power of Darkness* (*Vlast tmi*, 1887) was directed by Stanislavski at the Moscow Art Theatre, and performed at the Kamergerski Theatre in November 1902. See Stanislavski's *My Life in Art*, op. cit.

[36] Literally, Efros's use of '*an und für sich*' means 'in itself'.

[37] As far as Chekhov was concerned, Stanislavski *did* indulge himself with the sound effects, and this produced more than one wry comment in his letters. Writing about *Cherry Orchard* to his wife, Olga Knipper, Chekhov complained about Stanislavski: 'He wants to bring on a train in Act II, but I think he must be restrained. He also wants frogs and corncrakes' (23 November 1903). And on the same day he wrote to Stanislavski himself: 'If you can show a train without any noise, without a single sound, then carry on. . .' And on one of the rare occasions when Chekhov and Stanislavski were together, Chekhov made sure that Stanislavski over-heard him say: 'I shall write a new play and it will start with a character saying: "How wonderfully quiet it is! No birds to be heard, no dogs, no cuckoos, no owls, no nightingales, no clocks, no harness bells, and not a single cricket!"' This is disarmingly quoted by Stanislavski himself in *My Life in Art*, op. cit., p.420. And he adds: 'That stone was intended for my garden. . .'

[38] Mikhail Shchepkin (1788–1863), born a serf, was the greatest actor of his time. Initially 'the property' of Count Volkenstein, he acted as an amateur in the Count's rural theatre, but in 1808 was granted permission to become a professional. It was not until 1821 that he was given his freedom, and he then had a long and successful career at the Moscow Imperial Theatre where he specialized in character parts – and in creating a 'naturalistic school' of acting. Influenced by the quiet and restrained acting of the amateur actor, Prince Meshcherski, Shchepkin managed to rid himself of the 'old' methods of acting: shouting, mumbling in dialogues, and performing monologues with unrestrained pomposity – in short, the conventional acting style which bore little relation to observed reality. Essentially a comic actor he was also able to move his audience to tears, as well as laughter. His most famous roles were Famusov in Griboyedov's *Woe from Wit* (*Gore ot uma*, 1824) or *Wit Works Woe* (and other translations of the title), the Mayor in Gogol's masterpiece, *The Government Inspector* (*Revizor*, 1836), and the tragic character of old Kuzovkin in Turgenev's *The Parasite*. Raising the Maly Theatre – 'Moscow's Second University' – to the highest level of theatre art and craftsmanship, Shchepkin is known as 'the father of Russian realistic acting', influencing the reputation of the actor, and the art of acting, as well as such famous Russian actors as Sosnitski, Varlamov, Davidov, Sadovski, Fedotova and Yakovliev. Shchepkin's elevation of the art of theatre in turn elevated theatre criticism to a new level – such great writers and critics as Pushkin, Belinski, Herzen, Gogol, Aksakov and Viazemski, all wrote about and for Shchepkin and the theatre as an art and 'platform' for debate.

[39] It has subsequently been said with reference to Beckett's plays that the audience 'are Beckett characters in a Beckett situation'.

[40] Mstislav Dobuzhinski (1878–1958), with Benois and Diaghilev, a member of the famous 'The World of Art' Group of painters and designers. His setting for *A Month in the Country* (*Mesiats v derevne*, 1850) largely contributed to the production's success at the MAT in 1909. He was renowned as a designer working with many directors, including Evreinov, and was a consummate painter of St Petersburg scenes. Alexander Nikolaievich Benois (1870–1960) designed and directed at the Art Theatre from 1913–15. His refined art brought innovative scenography to ballet at the Imperial Mariinskii Theatre, and he designed and directed an extraordinarily sophisticated production of Pushkin's dramatic scenes for the MAT, as well as Goldoni's *La Locandiera* for Stanislavski. See Biographical Notes.

[41] Efros is directly quoting Trigorin in Act II of *Seagull*, at the end of the scene between

Trigorin and Nina – it is Nina who is 'the plot for a short story' for Trigorin – a prophetic telling of a story which has only taken place by Act IV of the play.

42 This is a digest of Nina's first speech in the play-within-the-play in Act I. In fact, cast and audience reacted in a similar way to Arkadina and most of the other on-stage characters.

43 Efros is referring to the revival in 1905, but which played only 11 performances before it was dropped by the Moscow Art Theatre – until 1960. See my introductory notes to this collection and Note 64. See E. Braun, *The Director and the Stage*, op. cit., p.65, and L. Senelick, *The Chekhov Theatre*, op. cit., chapter 2.

44 Hauptmann's play, written in 1890 and first performed in 1891, was much influenced by Ibsen's *Rosmersholm*. It is odd that Efros is so critical of Meyerhold since according to Stanislavski, Chekhov loved Meyerhold's performance as both Johannes Vockerat and Trepliov. Thus in *My Life in Art*, Stanislavski wrote: 'After the performance of "Lonely Lives" (sic) Chekhov showed a great deal of attention to one of the actors of our group, Vsevolod Meierhold (sic), who in his turn could not find words to express his admiration of Chekhov and Chekhov's writings. He played the leading parts of Treplev in "The Seagull" and Johannes in "Lonely Lives".' Stanislavski, op. cit. p.367. In J. Benedetti's *The Moscow Art Theatre Letters*, London: Methuen, 1991, Benedetti translates several letters of praise for Meyerhold the actor – from Chekhov's sister about his Trepliov (p.44), from Nemirovich-Danchenko ('Treplev – Meyerhold, graduated with highest honours. There have only ever been two like that. The other was Moskvin. . .', p.36), or Stanislavski's letter to Nemirovich of 30 August 1898 in which he explains his reliance on Meyerhold in helping him understand Chekhov (p.33). The only criticism is in a letter of 12 September 1898 from Nemirovich to Stanislavski, and during rehearsals of *Seagull*: 'Meyerhold at the beginning was all nerves and hysteria, which does not fit Chekhov's ideas at all, but now he has toned it down and is on the right track. The main trouble is that he was playing Act Four in Act One. You know?' (p.38). See also L. Senelick's *The Chekhov Theatre*, op. cit., in which he writes: 'Meyerhold's Treplev, which Nemirovich had shaped to be "tender, touching, an obvious degenerate," was praised for his fire, though some rather believed he overdid the sulphurous element. . .', pp.48–9, and see Senelick's note 90, p.369 and further evidence in opposition to Efros's view.

45 [Original footnote by Efros] Meyerhold, however, had one quality which was invaluable to the challenge of that first production of *Seagull*: he had a complete understanding and feel for Chekhov's work. Like the actress Nina Zarechnaya, he came on stage already imbued with Chekhov's poetry.

Talking about Meyerhold's performance as Vockerat [in Hauptmann's *Einsame Menschen*], Chekhov said that he loved Hauptmann's drama very much, partly due to Meyerhold who 'although not an infectious actor, makes one listen to him with pleasure because he understands everything he is saying'.

Meyerhold was able to influence the other actors over both of these plays, given his faith, his conviction, and even his love of Chekhov and Hauptmann. – Editor [Efros].

46 Efros had already described the inadequacies of Stanislavski's performance on page 12.

47 [Original footnote by Efros] In the spring of 1899, Chekhov came to Moscow – the famous group picture 'Chekhov with the *Seagull* 's performers' is from this period [see page 21 illustration 32: 'First read-through of *Seagull*']. Their Theatre was not working so they rented a theatre on Bolshaia Nikitskaia for the day (it was called 'the International' at that time) and they performed *Seagull* for Chekhov, but the performance had been prepared too hastily and did not have its full effect on the author. By the spring of 1900, Chekhov had not seen *Uncle Vanya*, and all the Theatre's requests for a new play were answered with refusals, and referred to the fact that he must see his plays performed by the Art Theatre for himself. Even if it were to result in loss, that is why the journey to Yalta was arranged. – Editor [Efros].

48 [Original footnote by Efros] The first act [of *Three Sisters*] was highly successful, and one of the Art Theatre's greatest successes. But then the audience's attitude changed and by the end, while it was satisfactory, it was less successful than the Theatre had expected. The same thing had happened with *Uncle Vanya* and was then to be repeated again with *Cherry Orchard*: it was only in the following season that there was a real success with a wider audience. – Editor [Efros].

49 The sense of optimism is not new to *Three Sisters*, nor the argument about melancholy. Efros himself quoted Chekhov's description of the play as 'a light comedy', and although it may be hard to play it that way, or to make it work in those terms, the argument relates to all of Chekhov's plays, and was a constant source of tension between the dramatist and the Art Theatre. See Notes 2, 20 and 30.

50 Hauptmann's play was produced by the Moscow Art Theatre in 1901, but was not well received.

51 The illustrations of the production show other actors in some of the parts: N.S. Butova as Olga; V.V. Baranovskaia as Irina; Podgorni as Fedotik, Berensev as Rode, but changing roles was common within the ensemble. See pp.42–53.

52 This highly unlikely subject for a play by Chekhov *was* confirmed by his wife, Olga Knipper, and is quoted by Ronald Hingley in greater detail in *A New Life of Chekhov*, op. cit.: 'The hero, a scholar, loves a woman who either fails to return his love or is unfaithful to him, whereupon he goes away to the far north.' And Hingley continues to quote Knipper's description: 'Act III was to take place on the deck of an ice-bound ship whence the lonely scholar-hero spied the ghost of his beloved flitting past against the background of the aurora borealis' (See Works, *Polnoe sobranie sochinenii i pisem*, ed. S.D. Balukhaty and others, Moscow: 1944–51, 20 volumes, Vol. 20, p.291). By this time (May 1904), Chekhov only had months to live, but it seems highly unlikely that he would have been serious about this melodramatic plot for a play. Nikolai Efros was such an admirer of Chekhov's work that he tended to be rather serious and literal-minded (not unlike Stanislavski in this respect). At the risk of being frivolous about Chekhov's ideas in the last few months of his life, it seems to *this* editor (Vera Gottlieb) that Chekhov was being mischievous and teasing. The plot is all too reminiscent of a letter Chekhov wrote to his friend and fellow-writer Kuprin: 'Why write that someone boards a submarine and sails to the North Pole to seek some sort of reconciliation with people, and at the same time his beloved, with a dramatic wail, throws herself from a belfry? All that is false and does not happen in reality. One must write simply: about how Peter Semeonovich married Maria Ivanovna. That's all.' Quoted in V. Gottlieb, *Chekhov and the Vaudeville*, op. cit., p.80. All of Chekhov's plays are about contemporary reality, and he only uses melodrama to expose the melodramatic in human behaviour.

53 Efros is no doubt referring to the miscarriage Olga Knipper suffered in March 1902 while on tour in St Petersburg with the Art Theatre. On 31 March she had an operation in a Petersburg clinic, and after two weeks of serious illness, was just well enough to travel to Yalta on the Sevastopol steamer, and then stretchered to the Chekhov house to join her extremely ill husband. In May both were well enough to travel to Moscow where Olga had a relapse, and at the beginning of June was diagnosed with peritonitis. It was not until the middle of June that she was well enough for Chekhov to leave her and travel to Perm, to stay with the Art Theatre's financial backer, S.I. (Savva) Morozov, a factory owner and landowner.

54 Efros was not being disingenuous about politics and *Cherry Orchard*. This was written and published by Efros in 1914, after the increased surveillance and censorship following the 1905 revolution, just months after Chekhov's death. There were three kinds of censorship in Tsarist Russia: State, Church and local or regional. Although the Art Theatre was a 'private' theatre as distinct from the Imperial Alexandrinski Theatre or Maly Theatre where the censorship was more stringent, nonetheless all performances, whether 'public' or 'private', were subject to strict censorship. Chekhov described it himself in these terms: 'It's like writing with a bone stuck in your throat.' Ambivalence or oblique writing was not just a characteristic of the Chekhovian style, but a way of getting round the censorship. For detailed descriptions of problems with the censors over Chekhov's plays, see R. Hingley, *The Oxford Chekhov* in 3 volumes, or his *A New Life of Chekhov*, and several collections of letters available in English, Note 30. See also V. Gottlieb, 'The "Dwindling Scale": The Politics of British Chekhov' in P. Miles, ed., *Chekhov on the British Stage*, Cambridge: CUP, 1993. See also E. Polotskaya, 'Chekhov and his Russia' in V. Gottlieb & P. Allain, eds *The Cambridge Companion to Chekhov*, Cambridge: CUP, 2000. Also, crucially, W.H. Bruford, *Chekhov and his Russia, A Sociological Study*, London: Routledge & Kegan Paul Ltd., 1948 & reissued 1971.

55 Efros indicates quite clearly here that he understands the 'political' implications of and in the play, yet remains within the bounds of the permissible or publishable. He is less clear, however, about the 'optimistic' or positive elements in the other plays.

56 This does read very much in terms of post-1905 Russia, written the year World War I broke out, and three years before the revolutions of 1917. It is difficult to interpret what Efros writes in any other way.

57 Although Chekhov was by this time irritable and edgy from illness, he was able to see rehearsals of the play (in December), and was profoundly depressed by it. He *did* regret the fact that Stanislavski played Gayev – see letter of 14 October 1903 in which he wrote: 'Gayev is for Vishnevski'; on 30 October 1903 to Knipper: 'The part of Lopakhin is the central one. If it doesn't come off, the whole play will be ruined. . .'; and to Stanislavski on the same day: 'When I wrote the part of Lopakhin I wrote it as your part. . . If for some reason you don't like the look of it, then play Gayev. . .' Other letters of this period are full of detailed directions about the play as a whole and about the individual characters, in particular Lopakhin and Ranevskaya, but after the first performance on 17 January 1904, Chekhov was profoundly disappointed by the Art Theatre's production. On 29 March, four months before his death, he wrote to Knipper: 'The only thing I can say is that Stanislavski has ruined my play. Well, the less I say about him the better. . .' Chekhov is referring to the interpretation of the play as a whole, but he was dissatisfied with much of the casting. Lopakhin was played by Massalitinov. See Illustrations on pp.55–70. See also R. Hingley, *The Oxford Chekhov*, Vol. 3, op. cit.

58 Chekhov's funeral carried with it the same mix of 'sad comicality of everyday life' that was uniquely his style – or, to put it another way, the combination of the tragic and trivial. First, the huge grieving crowd which met the train carrying Chekhov's body to St Petersburg, discovered that it was carried in a wagon labelled 'fresh oysters'. When an equally huge crowd met the train in Moscow, they initially followed the wrong hearse (of a general), and then realized in time to inter the body at the Novodevichi Monastery, next to Chekhov's father.

59 Like Hamlet, Ivanov cracks under the weight of conscience and – in the Russian version of 'Hamletism' – also under the weight of the contemporary way of life which sapped and then destroyed the will and energy of many educated and thinking Russians. See Note 18 for a more detailed explanation and examples. See the stories *In Moscow* (or 'A Moscow Hamlet') or *Three Years*, while the dire effect may be seen in such stories as *Man in a Case* or in many characters in the plays whether in the one-act *The Wedding*, or in the character of Vanya, or Andrei in *Three Sisters*. Efros's point is perhaps clarified by the quotation: 'In the land of the blind, the one-eyed

man is king.' Youthful, energetic and progressive people start off full of hope and the wish to change their contemporary reality, but are defeated by the sheer size of the challenge and weight of the burden they take upon themselves. For the audience of *Ivanov*, the central character was an immediately recognizable and identifiable 'type' – not hysterical or eccentric but depressed, exhausted from the defeat of idealism and hope. In Chekhov's treatment and clearly expressed opinions, this was sometimes a dramatic or serious but not a tragic figure.

60 The Imperial Censorship Committee for Theatre and Literature.

61 [Original footnote by Nemirovich-Danchenko] By the way, the newspapers accused me of being one of the members of the Theatrical and Literary Committee which sat at the Imperial Maly Theatre, and that I therefore took part in the censorship of *Uncle Vanya*. I have already often repudiated this myth, and allow myself the opportunity to repeat here what actually happened. I was a member of the Theatrical-Literary Committee for seven years until the opening of the Art Theatre. When it was finally decided by myself and K.S. Stanislavski in the spring of 1898 that from the autumn we would have our own Theatre, I declared to V.A. Telyakovski, the director of the Imperial Theatre, that it was no longer possible for me to remain on the Theatrical-Literary Committee. V.A. Telyakovski had only just begun his administration, and he asked me not to resign officially until he had found someone to replace me. I agreed, but declared that I would not attend the sessions of the Committee. And then, according to the official facts which I have previously cited in the newspapers, I attended only one session in the course of the winter – that November – at which I handed over the plays which had been in my possession since the previous year. Since then I have neither attended a single session nor received any fee. – V.I. Nemirovich-Danchenko.

62 See Page 21, Illustration 32. This studio photograph of the first read-through of *Seagull* is often reproduced, whereas the reaction to the play in the following Illustration 33, is known but not as frequently published.

63 On 9 January, a day subsequently known as 'Bloody Sunday', a peaceful demonstration of unarmed workers asking for better conditions, was violently attacked in the huge square outside the Tsar's Winter Palace in St Petersburg by the Tsar's Winter Palace cavalry guard. The official figure of deaths was recorded as 700 demonstrators, but there were probably more 'lost' under the ice. This triggered the 1905 armed uprising which was brutally suppressed. The reaction of many of the progressive intelligentsia was that of deep depression at the failure of the revolution, and one of the 'casualties' was the Moscow Art Theatre's financial backer, Savva Morozov, who left for Nice, and shot himself there. He had already withdrawn all but minimal financial support since he sided with Gorki over a row between Gorki and Nemirovich-Danchenko. See end of Note 67.

64 See Note 70. The MAT did not reinstate *Seagull* until Viktor Stanitsin's 1960 production, and then again in 1968 in a production by Boris Livanov. This production played at London's Aldwych Theatre in May 1970, as part of that year's World Theatre Season. See Appendix 2: *Select Stage Productions* in V. Gottlieb and P. Allain, eds, *The Cambridge Companion to Chekhov*, Cambridge: CUP, 2000. There had been other Russian productions before then, the most original being the production at Moscow's Lenin-Komsomol Theatre by Anatoly Efros (no relation to Nikolai Efros) in 1966. See L. Senelick, *The Chekhov Theatre: A century of the play in performance*, Cambridge: CUP, 1997, for a detailed index of all of Chekhov's plays in (professional) performance in Russia and elsewhere, pp.414–21.

65 See Note 8 on Alexei Tolstoi's trilogy. The Moscow Art Theatre did *Tsar Fiodor* in October 1898; Shakespeare's *Julius Caesar* in October 1903, and Ibsen's *Brand* in December 1906. Stanislavski writes about the productions in *My Life in Art*, London: Geoffrey Bles, 1962 (from first publication in 1948, copyright Elizabeth Reynolds Hapgood, USA). See Note 7.

66 The Black Sea city and port of Sevastopol is best-known to British readers and historians from the Crimean War. By the time of Chekhov's 'exile' in the Crimea, Sevastopol had access by rail, sea and road, and was the largest city close to Yalta. If travelling from Moscow by train, it requires transferring from rail to road transport to get down the mountains to Yalta. Alternatively, people travelled by steamer to and from Yalta and Sevastopol, but the largest Black Sea port was and remains Odessa.

67 The Moscow Art Theatre premiered Gorki's *Philistines (Meshtchane)* while on tour in St Petersburg on 26 March 1902. This is translated in the Hapgood American version of Stanislavski's *My Life in Art* as *Small People*, and the premiere given as October 1902. The play has also been translated as *The Petty Bourgeois*.

Gorki's *Lower Depths (Na dne)* was then premiered by the Moscow Art Theatre in December 1902. See a description of the premiere of *Philistines* by Edward Braun in his introduction to *Gorky*, *Five Plays*, London: Methuen, 1988, pp.xvi–xvii, although the play itself is not in the collection.

It is significant that Chekhov wrote of *Philistines*: 'Gorki is the first in Russia and in the world at large to have expressed contempt and loathing for the petty bourgeoisie and he has done it at the precise moment when Russia is ready for protest'. Braun, p.xvii. Chekhov had himself exposed the same milieu in, for example, his own one-act plays *The Wedding* (1889–1890), and *The Anniversary* or *Jubilee* (1891); in the treatment of Natasha in *Three Sisters*, as well as in numerous short stories.

Gorki was deeply impressed by the Moscow Art Theatre's production of *Seagull* and after seeing their production of *Uncle Vanya* he described it as 'music, not acting', Gorki (21—8 March 1901), quoted in E.D. Surkov, ed., *Chekhov i teatr: pisma, feletoni, sovremenniki o Chekhove-dramaturge*, Moscow: Iskusstvo, 1961, p.362. Gorki was also well aware of the darker side of Chekhov's characterization, and not only the common view of his compassionate characterization. Gorki was initially more critical of the value of Chekhov's plays after the 1917 Revolutions – particularly with reference to the 1918–19 MAT season in which *Ivanov* was revived, not the most immediately relevant of plays for that time. But in 1928, when the Art Theatre followed a reinterpreted *Uncle Vanya* with a new interpretation of *Cherry Orchard*, Gorki (rightly) criticized the MAT for continuing to play it as a drama, and not as the comedy which Chekhov himself had ascribed in his subtitle.

68 Efros goes on to explain many of the cast changes within this introduction to the premiere production. Thus, for example, Olga was later played by Butova; Irina by Baranovskaia; Tuzenbakh by Kachalov, a part shared by Meyerhold which Efros does not mention. Such cast changes are common with any permanent company, but the cast-list at the top does not always correspond to the cast in the illustrations.

69 In a letter of 14 October 1888, Chekhov wrote: 'Between the big play and the one-act play, the difference is only quantitative. You too should write a vaudeville', and he wrote by the word 'vaudeville': 'a one-act drama or comedy'. In his vaudevilles, Chekhov erased the distinction between 'comedy' and 'drama' – a distinction which he also erased from his full-length plays. This is crucial to an understanding of his own views on his plays, and their misinterpretation by Stanislavski and many subsequent directors. Quoted in V. Gottlieb, *Chekhov and the Vaudeville*, Cambridge: CUP, 1982, pp.44–5. And see Notes 2, 30, 67 and 68.

70 Efros is again referring to the dismal failure of the St Petersburg Aleksandrinski Theatre production on 17 October 1896.

71 As many letters of the period show, Chekhov was also deeply concerned with the Art Theatre's interpretation of his comedy – and, as it turned out, with cause; with his own ideas over casting, and other elements with which he had been unhappy in the productions of his previous plays. His clashes with Stanislavski not only continued with *Cherry Orchard* but were further aggravated.

72 This is over-simplifying the arguments over casting, interpretation, tone and, for example, the usual disagreements over sound effects. For details, see several collections of letters, cited in Notes 7, 19 and 30. For previous commentary on *Cherry Orchard*, see Notes 30, 37, 48 and 54. See R. Hingley, Appendix IV, *The Cherry Orchard* in *The Oxford Chekhov*, Vol. 3, op. cit.

73 Efros is expressing similar views on Chekhov's 'realism' to those later defined by Nemirovich-Danchenko. See Note 31.

74 Efros rather confusingly suddenly uses a diminutive of the name. Samarova played Zinaida, Lebedev's wife and Sasha's mother.

75 As distinct from Chekhov's highly successful one-act plays such as *The Bear (Medved*, 1888) or *The Proposal (Predlozhenie*, 1888–89) or *The Anniversary* (or translated as *Jubilee*, *Yubiley*, 1891), among others. These were produced in Korsh's Theatre in Moscow, and then all over Russia, and their *seeming* conventionality ensured both their success and popularity. In fact, Chekhov develops many of the techniques he uses in the full-length plays by subverting the vaudeville genre to make innovatory use of the form. Thus he uses melodrama to expose the melodramatic in *The Proposal* as he does in *Seagull* or *Uncle Vanya*; he uses farce in *The Bear* and several others of the one-act plays as he then does in *Uncle Vanya* and *Cherry Orchard* – the obvious example in the former is Vanya's traditional entrance with the flowers, interrupting Astrov and Elena; or Vanya's tragi-comic failure to shoot Serebriakov three times at close range; or Yepikhodov in *Cherry Orchard*, whose misfortunes are both pure farce and a philosophical comment on his life. Thus in the one-act plays such as *The Wedding (Svadba*, 1889–90) or *On the Harmfulness of Tobacco (O vrede tabaka*, last version in 1903, also translated as *The Evils of Tobacco* or Hingley's *Smoking is Bad for You*), and in the full-length plays, farce often becomes a philosophical concept as well as a theatrical device, and in much of his work, including many short stories, it is the 'sad comicality of everyday life' which he exposes. For detailed comment on the one-act plays and their relation to his full-length plays, see V. Gottlieb, *Chekhov and the Vaudeville*, op. cit, or V. Gottlieb's 'Chekhov's one-act plays and the full-length plays', and D. Rayfield, 'Chekhov's stories and the plays' in V. Gottlieb & P. Allain, eds, *The Cambridge Companion to Chekhov*, op. cit. Here, however, Efros is writing about the dramatization of some short stories, and not the one-act plays which he does not mention anywhere in this publication – a common yet significant omission since the one-act plays have often been under-rated while innovatory and yet immensely popular and frequently performed.

76 Since then, Chekhov's short stories have often been dramatized and staged both in Russia and abroad. See P. Miles, ed., *Chekhov on the British Stage*, Cambridge: CUP, 1993, Appendix: *A selective chronology of British professional productions of Chekhov's plays 1909–1991*; V. Gottlieb, *A Chekhov Quartet* (consisting of two one-act plays, *On the Harmfulness of Tobacco (O vrede tabaka*, six versions from 1886 to 1902–03) and *Swan Song (Lebedinaya pesnya, Kalkhas*, 1887–88) and two short stories, *A Moscow Hamlet (V Moskve*, 1891) and *Accounts (Razmaznya*, 1883, literally translated as *Nincompoop* and variously as *Gormless* or *Day of Reckoning*). See R. Hingley, *The One Act Plays*, in *The Oxford Chekhov*, Vol. 1, Oxford: 1968, and D. Rayfield, *Chekhov, The Evolution of his Art*, London: Paul Elek, 1975.

BIOGRAPHICAL NOTES

Vera Gottlieb and Nick Worrall

Entries followed by name in square brackets and in bold are the original names as distinct from stage names or names changed for other reasons; entries with the same name in round brackets and not in bold relate to the most common English usage or differences in transliteration.

Abramova, Mariia Moritsovna [Geinrikh] (1865–92) actress and entrepreneur who in 1889 created one of the first private theatres, her own Abramova Theatre, following the rescinding of the Imperial monopoly in 1882 and where she staged Chekhov's *The Wood Demon* (unsuccessfully) in the theatre's first year.

Adabashian, Aleksandr (born 1945) together with the film's director, Nikita Mikhalkov-Konchalovski, he wrote the screenplay for *Unfinished Piece for Mechanical Piano* (1976) based on Chekhov's *Platonov*.

Adashev, Aleksandr Ivanovich [Platonov] (1871–1934) founder member of Moscow Art Theatre company 1898–1913. Actor and teacher at his own private theatre school, which he opened in 1906.

Aksakov, Sergei Timofeevich (1791–1859) writer, memoirist, narrator of his contemporary (end of 18th century) Russian life and society. Wrote on fishing, hunting, family life and customs. Reminiscences include works on Gogol, St Petersburg literary and theatrical life.

Alekseev, Konstantin Sergeevich – see Stanislavski.

Aleksandrov, Nikolai Grigorevich (1870–1930) member of Stanislavski's Society of Art and Literature, he joined the Moscow Art Theatre in 1898 and remained there until his death. Played Yasha in first production of *The Cherry Orchard* (1904).

Andreev, Leonid Nikolaevich (Andreyev, 1871–1919) playwright, prose writer and publicist. Plays include *The Life of Man* (1906–08) and *Anathema* (1909), produced at the Art Theatre. Famous play *He Who Gets Slapped* (1915). As 'Dzheims Linch' (James Lynch), Andreev wrote two essays on the MAT's production of *Three Sisters*.

Andreeva, Mariia Fedorovna [Zheliabuzhskaia] (1868–1953) actress with the Art Theatre, 1898–1904 and 1905–06. After an affair with Gorki, then became his second wife. Andreeva clashed constantly with Stanislavski.

Antoine, André (1858–1943) French actor and director who founded the Théâtre Libre where, from 1887 to 1894, he staged the latest examples of Naturalist and realist drama – by Ibsen, Strindberg, Hauptmann and others. Created his own Théâtre Antoine in 1897.

Artem, Aleksandr Rodionovich [Artemev] (1842–1914) a founder members of the MAT company. Parts included Shamrayev in *Seagull*; Telegin (Waffles) in *Uncle Vanya*, Chebutykin in *Three Sisters* and Firs in *Cherry Orchard*. He was also a drawing master and engraver.

Baliev, Nikita Fedorovich (1877–1936) actor and director at the Moscow Art Theatre, 1906–11, he made a name for himself at the famous 'cabbage' parties' as a cabaret performer and later founded his own cabaret theatre *Letuchaia mysh* (The Flying Bat, or Fledermaus) in 1920.

Baranovskaia Vera Vsevolodna (1885–1935) a member of the Moscow Art Theatre company from 1903 to 1915, she emigrated in 1928. Took over the role of Irina in *Three Sisters* after Andreeva and Litovtseva.

Beckett, Samuel Barclay (1906–89) Irish novelist and playwright who lived in France from the late 1930s until his death and who became world famous when his *En Attendant Godot* (*Waiting for Godot*, 1953) was his first play to be performed.

Belinski, Vissarion Grigorevich (1811–48). first professional Russian critic, his writings on Pushkin, Lermontov, Griboedov, Gogol, Dostoevski, Turgenev, Goncharov and Nekrasov, helped ensure their place in Russian classical literature. Set a standard and criteria for radical literary criticism which continued into the 20th century.

Benua, Aleksandr Nikolaevich [Alexandre Benois] (1870–1960) designed and directed at the MAT, 1913–15. Designed ballets at the Mariinskii Theatre. Founder member of World of Art Group (Mir Iskusstva) with impresario Diaghilev for whom he designed productions for the Ballet Russes. Scenographer, critic and art historian.

Benson, Frank (1858–1939) English actor manager whose career was spent performing Shakespeare at Stratford-upon-Avon and touring Shakespearean productions around Britain as well as visiting the United States, Canada and South Africa.

Bersenev, Ivan Nikolaevich [Pavlishchev] (1889–1951) acted at the Moscow Art Theatre, 1911–24, before joining MAT2 in 1924 and becoming its artistic director, 1928–36 .

Brahm, Otto (1856–1912) German critic and theatre manager who co-founded the *Freie Bühne* (Free Stage) in Berlin in 1889 modelled on the example of Antoine's *Théâtre Libre*.

Bulgakov, Mikhail Afanasevich (1891–1940) playwright, novelist, doctor. The MAT staged *Days of the Turbins*, 1926 from his novel *The White Guard* 1924; *Flight*, completed 1927 unperformed in lifetime; *A Cabal of Hypocrites* or *Molièr* (1936, after four years' rehearsal, only seven performances). Plays banned. 1929. Assistant director at MAT, 1930–36; dramatized Gogol's *Dead Souls* (1932). *Black Snow* (*Teatral'ny roman/A Theatrical Novel/Romance*, 1936–37), a parody of Stanislavski and the MAT.

Butova, Nadezhda Sergeevna (1878–1921) a pupil of Nemirovich-Danchenko's at the Moscow Philharmonic School, Butova joined the Moscow Art Theatre in 1900 where she remained until her death. Played Babakina in *Ivanov* (1904) and took over the role of Olga in *Three Sisters* from Savitskaia.

Chekhov, Aleksandr Pavlovich (1855–1913) first born of Pavel (shopkeeper) and Evgeniia Chekhov; Anton Chekhov's older brother. All Chekhov siblings were grandchildren of emancipated serf. Wrote a memoir of the Chekhovs and of his famous writer brother. Literary gifts squandered by alcoholism. Father of famous actor/producer Mikhail (Michael) Chekhov.

Chekhov, Anton Pavlovich (1860–1904) doctor, playwright, author of popular short stories. Chekhov set up schools, libraries, clinics, and undertook arduous journey to the prison island of Sakhalin where he conducted a survey which was published and resulted in some important penal reform. Plays internationally performed. Married to actress Olga Knipper.

Chekhov, Ivan Pavlovich (1861–1922) fourth of the Chekhov brothers. Teacher.

Chekhova, Mariia Pavlovna (1863–1957) Chekhov's sister curator and guardian of his work and house in Yalta where she lived until her death.

Chekhov, Michael [Mikhail Aleksandrovich] (1891–1955) actor, director, theorist and nephew of the playwright, Chekhov acted at the Moscow Art Theatre and its Studios during the early 1920s before becoming artistic director of MAT2. He emigrated in 1928 and established acting studios in England and America where he taught his own version of Stanislavski's 'system'.

Chronegk, Ludwig (1837–91) director for the Duke of Saxe-Meiningen and his innovatory theatre company. Emphasis on historical accuracy, individualized crowd scenes, realistic staging, and the new roles of director and designer.

Davydov, Vladimir Nikolaevich [Gorelov, Ivan] (1849–1925). actor at the Aleksandrinski Theatre. Chekhov wrote lead role in *Swan Song (Kalkhas* 1886–87) for him (Korsh's Theatre, Moscow, 1888). Played title role in *Ivanov*, January 1889, at Korsh's Theatre; then at the St Petersburg Aleksandrinski Theatre, 1889.

Diaghilev, Sergei Pavlovich [Diagilev] (1872–1929) producer, impresario, journalist, musician. Creator of the Ballet Russes. Founder member with Aleksandr Benois of World of Art Group, 1898–1904. Organized exhibitions of Russian and Western European contemporary art.

Dmitrevskaia, Liubov Ivanovna (1890–?) acted at the Moscow Art Theatre from 1906 to 1924.

Dobuzhinski, Mstislav (1878–1958) with Benois and Diaghilev, member of the famous World of Art Group. Designed Turgenev's *A Month in the Country* (*Mesiats v derevne*, 1850) for the Moscow Art Theatre in 1909 and renowned as a designer working for many directors, including Evreinov. Painted scenes of St Petersburg.

Dreyfus, Alfred (1854–1935) Jewish Captain in French Army. Accusation of treason resulted in imprisonment on French Devil's Island. Émile Zola and other European progressives (including Chekhov) considered him an innocent object of anti-Semitism. Controversial issue between reactionaries and progressives. Found innocent and released after major scandal in French army and government.

Efros, Anatoli Vasilevich (1925–87) Soviet director who came to prominence during the 1960s with controversial productions staged at the Moscow Theatre on Malaia Bronnaia. He succeeded Yuri Liubimov at the Taganka Theatre in 1984 following Liubimov's decision not to return to the Soviet Union.

Efros, Nikolai Efimovich (1867–1923) law graduate, journalist, theatre critic, literary manager of the MAT. Author of monographs on Stanislavski, (1918) on *Three Sisters* and *Cherry Orchard* (1919), *History of Russian Theatre* (1914), *The Moscow Art Theatre, 1898–1923*, (1923). Editor of this collection of the plays of Chekhov at the Moscow Art Theatre, 1914.

Ermolova – see Yermolova.

Evreinov, Nikolai Nikolaevich (1879–1953) Russian director, theorist and theatre historian who directed plays at the satirical 'Crooked Mirror' Theatre in St Petersburg before the revolution and who later staged 'The Storming of the Winter Palace' as a mass open-air spectacle in 1920 before emigrating to France in 1925.

Fedorov, Fedor Aleksandrovich [Yurkovski] (1842–1915) director at the Aleksandrinski Theatre, St Petersburg, 1864–96.

Fedotova, Glikeria Nikolaevna (1846–1925) actress, teacher of Stanislavski. Leading actress at the Moscow Maly Theatre, 1862–1905.

Franz, Ellen (1839–1923) wife of Duke Georg of Saxe-Meiningen (1826–1914) who worked with him when they created their own (professional) theatre company. Touring Europe, they influenced Stanislavski, André Antoine, Otto Brahm, G.T. Grein, among others, given their historical accuracy in productions, individualized crowd scenes, and the emerging roles of director and designer.

Germanova, Mariia Nikolaevna [Krasovskaia] (1884–1940) actress member of the MAT company, 1902–19, when she emigrated while on tour.

Gertsen – see Herzen.

Glama-Meshcherskaia, Aleksandra Iakovlevna [Barisheva] (1859–1942) Maly Theatre actress.

Gogol, Nikolai Vasilevich (1809–52) Russia's greatest 19th-century comic writer, of novels, short stories and plays. Ukrainian by birth, Gogol lived in St Petersburg but mostly abroad. The ideas for two of his most famous works, the comic play *The Government Inspector* or *The Inspector General* (1836) and the novel *Dead Souls* (1842), were credited by Gogol to his mentor and friend Pushkin. The play was an immediate success, produced ever since. The MAT staged the play in 1908 and produced Bulgakov's dramatization of *Dead Souls* in 1932.

Goltsev, Viktor Alexandrovich (1850–1906) journalist, critic, editor.

Gorich, Nikolai Nikolaevich [Vishnevetski] (1877–1949) acted at the Moscow Art Theatre between 1906 and 1911. Took over the role of the stationmaster in *The Cherry Orchard*, a character whom Stanislavski introduced into Act Three of the play.

Gorki, Maksim (Maxim Gorky) **[Peshkov, Aleksei Maksimovich]** (1868–1936) Russian dramatist, short-story writer and novelist. Friend of Chekhov's. His first plays were performed at the Moscow Art Theatre, most famously *Philistines* and *Lower Depths* (both 1902). Political activist and exile, Tolstoi called him 'a real man of the people'. Gorki chose to live abroad during the 1920s, returning to the Soviet Union in the early 1930s. Became a leading advocate of Soviet 'socialist realism' after 1934.

Grein, J.T. (1862–1935) Dutch playwright and theatre manager who became a British citizen and founded the Independent Theatre Society in London in 1891 modelled on Antoine's Théâtre Libre.

Griboedov, Aleksandr Sergeevich (Griboyedov 1795–1829) diplomat and dramatist. Among many vaudevilles and satires, Griboedov's most famous play is the biting *Woe from Wit* (or *The Misfortune of Being Clever*, 1823–24, only published in full, 1861), with the leading character, Chatski, a 'characteristic type' in Russian literature and society.

Griboyedov's progressive ideas resulted in arrest (after the Decembrist uprising) and strict censorship. The MAT produced the play in 1906.

Gribunin, Vladimir Fedorovich (1873–1933). renowned actor and founder member of the MAT company.

Griffiths, Trevor (1935–) English playwright who came to prominence in 1973 when his play about the student revolution of 1968, *The Party*, was staged at the English National Theatre. He adapted Chekhov's *The Cherry Orchard* for the stage in 1977.

Grigorev, Mikhail Grigorevich (no dates available) acted at the Moscow Art Theatre for a single season 1899–1900.

Grigoreva, Mariia Petrovna [Nikolaeva] (1869–1941) acted at Stanislavski's Society of Art and Literature and joined the Moscow Art Theatre at its inception where she remained until her death. She also managed the costume department of the First Studio.

Gromov, Mikhail Apollinarevich (?–1918) acted at the Moscow Art Theatre from 1899 to 1906. Played Solioni in first production of *Three Sisters* (1901).

Hauptmann, Gerhart (1862–1946) German 'naturalist' and symbolist playwright. Four of his plays staged by the MAT, including *Lonely Lives*, (*Einsame Menschen – Lonely People*, 1890), in 1891, with Meyerhold playing Johannes Vockerat, translated by Nikolai Efros and, unsuccessfully, *Michael Kramer* (1900).

Herzen, Aleksandr Ivanovich [Gertsen] (1812–70) writer, journalist, editor, philosopher. Part of literary group including Goncharov, Turgenev and Dostoevsky, wrote fiction, philosophy, essays. After arrest and exile, he then left Russia after 1847 and his work expressed the most influential socio-political ideas in 19th-century Russian intellectual life. Herzen worked with the radical Belinsky, but Herzen's more liberal views were expressed in *Who Is to Blame?*(1845–47) and memoirs *My Past and Thoughts* (1852–68). Lived for a while in Putney, London. In his trilogy *The Coast of Utopia* (2002), Tom Stoppard uses Herzen, Belinsky and Bakunin to explore ideas and reactions to the revolutions of 1848.

Hugo, Victor (1802–95) French novelist, poet and dramatist. His verse dramas, such as *Cromwell* (1827) were written in high Romantic style. His first performed play, *Hernani* (1830) caused riots and ushered in a new era in French theatre. Several novels were staged and have often been filmed – the best-known being *Les Misérables*.

Ibsen, Henrik (1828–1906) Norwegian dramatist who also worked as a stage director before becoming a full-time playwright. Left Norway for Italy during the 1860s where he wrote his verse dramas *Brand* and *Peer Gynt*. Returning to Northern Europe, Ibsen pioneered the realist drama of the late 19th century with plays of middle-class domesticity which were received with a mixture of critical rapture and moral outrage.

Kachalov, Vasili Ivanovich [Shverubovich] (1875–1948) Kachalov became the leading actor after Stanislavski when he joined the Art Theatre in 1900. Kachalov took over and 'ennobled' the role of Tuzenbakh when Meyerhold left, subsequently playing Trofimov in the premiere of *Cherry Orchard* and the title role in *Ivanov*, 1904, directed by Nemirovich-Danchenko. Versatile and subtle, one of Kachalov's strengths as an actor was his voice. He is regarded as one of Russia's greatest actors.

Khaliutina, Sofia Vasilevna (1875–1960) a former pupil of Nemirovich-Danchenko at the Moscow Philharmonic School, she acted and taught at the Moscow Art Theatre between 1898 and 1950. Played Dunyasha in the first production of *The Cherry Orchard* (1904) and later acted the role of Charlotta.

Knipper-Chekhova, Olga Leonardovna (1868–1959) actress at the Art Theatre from its foundation until her death. Student and mistress of Nemirovich-Danchenko, she immediately played leading roles. On 16 June 1899 started correspondence with Chekhov which finally filled three large volumes. Eventually married on 25 May 1901, there were long periods of separation with Chekhov in Yalta and Knipper acting in Moscow or on tour. Of German background, she married Chekhov in a Russian Orthodox Church. Knipper was famed among other roles for her creation of *Seagull*'s Arkadina, Elena in *Uncle Vanya*, Masha in *Three Sisters*, Ranevskaya in *Cherry Orchard* and Sasha in *Ivanov*, not always the parts Chekhov planned for her.

Komissarzhevskaia, Vera Fedorovna (1864–1910) actress, director of her own theatre in St Petersburg, 1904. Half-sister of famous director, designer Fedor Komissarzhevski (Fiodor – Theodore). Worked briefly with Stanislavski. Then joined St Petersburg Aleksandrinski Theatre where she played the first Nina in the disastrous premiere of *Seagull* (1896). Employed Meyerhold as artistic director of her theatre, 1906–08. Highly popular actress.

Koni, Anatoli Fedorovich (1844–1927) liberal jurist and memoirist. Famously acquitted Vera Zasulich in 1878, tried for attempted murder of reactionary tsarist general Trepov. After Revolution, Lunacharski awarded Koni law professorship at (then) Petrograd University. Famous five-volume memoirs *On the Path of Life* (1913–29).

Kondratev, Aleksei Mikhailevich (1846–1913) actor, then chief director at the Maly Theatre, 1901–07.

Koreneva, Lidiia Mikhailovna (1885–?) acted at the Moscow Art Theatre from 1904 to 1958.

Korsh, Fedor Adamovich (1852–1923) critic, dramatist, impresario of his own Moscow Korsh Theatre, 1882, taken over from Anna Brenko's Pushkin Theatre. Shrewd mix of commercialism and experiment, including new plays by Ibsen, Lev Tolstoi, and Friday matinee reduced prices for students. Chekhov's *Ivanov* was first staged, disastrously, at Korsh's Theatre in 1887, directed by Agramov, and taken off after three performances. Several of Chekhov's one-act plays were staged there – *The Evils of Tobacco* or *On the Harmfulness of Tobacco*, 1886; *Swan Song (Kalkhas)*, 1887 and *The Bear* 1888

Kosminskaia, Liubov Aleksandrovna (1880–1946) joined the Moscow Art Theatre Acting School in 1901 and remained with the company until 1915.

Kozintsev, Grigori Mikhailovich (1905–73) Russian stage and film director best known for his creation of The Factory of the Eccentric Actor in post-revolutionary Leningrad and for his films of *Hamlet* (1964) and *King Lear* (1971).

Kugel, Aleksandr Rafailovich (1864–1928) theatre critic and reviewer for *The Petersburg Newspaper*. Kugel misunderstood Chekhov's plays, mocking the first unfortunate production at the Imperial Aleksandrinski Theatre with Komissarzhevskaia, subsequently deriding the MAT productions of *Seagull* and *Uncle Vanya*. In particular, he wrote of Olga Knipper: 'Praise of this actress is an utter mystery to me.' Nikolai Efros describes Kugel as 'an enemy of the Art Theatre' but even Kugel was eventually less biased and more perceptive.

Kuprin, Aleksandr Ivanovich (1870–1938) novelist. With Gorky, Andreev and Bunin, member of the 'Znanie' ('Knowledge') writers' group. Novellas, short stories and novels depict contemporary social evils, but he also wrote factual stories, such as his *Kiev Types* – depictions of army life and romantic stories. Emigrated to France after the Revolution, returning to Leningrad in 1937.

Lavrentev, Andrei Nikolaevich (1882–1935) joined the Moscow Art Theatre Acting School in 1902 and remained with the company until 1910.

Lavrov, Vukol Mikhailovich (1852–1912) liberal co-editor with V.A. Goltsev of *Russian Thought (Russkaia/Russkaya mysl)*. Chekhov almost accused Lavrov of libel, ending relations in 1890. This was symptomatic of Chekhov's endless battle with critics and reviewers given his hatred of hypocritical condescension and 'high-minded' pretentious criticism. By 1892 friendship was re-established, and Chekhov gave them the famous story *Ward Number Six* in November 1892, followed by first publication of 13 stories, *Sakhalin Island*, and both *Seagull* and *Three Sisters*.

Lenin, Vladimir Ilich [Ulianov] (1870–1924) Russian revolutionary leader of the Bolsheviks and chief theoretician of Russian Marxism, he led the forces of the October revolution in 1917 and laid the basis for the New Economic Policy of the 1920s.

Lenski, Dmitri Timofeevich [Vorobev] (1805 [?1809]–60) Maly Theatre actor and author of around one hundred plays, mainly 'vaudevilles', the most famous being *Lev Gurich Sinichkin* (1839).

Lenski, Aleksandr Pavlovich [Verbitsiotti] (1847–1908) actor, director and teacher at the Moscow Maly Theatre from 1876 until his death. The Maly's production of Chekhov's *Wood Demon* was planned as a benefit performance for Lenski, but Lenski returned the script, offensively suggesting Chekhov should never write plays.

Leonidov, Leonid Mironovich (1873–1941) director and actor who joined the MAT in 1903. Among other major roles, he played Soleny (Solioni) in the premiere of *Three Sisters*; played Lopakhin in premiere of *Cherry Orchard* and played Borkin in *Ivanov*.

Lepkovski, Evgeni Arkadevich (1863–1939) served a season at the Moscow Art Theatre between 1901 and 1902.

Levitan, Isaak Ilich (1860–1900) the great Russian landscape artist and close friend of Chekhov's through his painter brother Nikolai. Levitan's landscapes create mood and atmosphere, and capture both the grandeur of the Russian countryside and the beauty of details. Worked with Diaghilev as a set designer.

Lilina, Mariia Petrovna [Perevoshchikova] [Alekseeva] (1856–1943) renowned MAT actress, who first played Masha in *Seagull*, Sonia in *Uncle Vanya*, Natasha in *Three Sisters*, Varya in *Cherry Orchard* and many other leading MAT roles. Stanislavski's [Alekseev's] wife.

Litovtseva, Nina Nikolaevna [Lewenstamm] (1878–1956) actress with the MAT from 1901. Married the great MAT actor Vasili Kachalov. Litovtseva then worked at the MAT's Second Studio.

Livanov, Boris Nikolaevich (1904–72) actor and director at the Moscow Art Theatre from 1924 until his death. His production of *The Seagull* was seen at the World Theatre Season in London in 1970.

Los, Anton Potapovich (?–1914) acted at the Moscow Art Theatre, 1904–06.

Lunacharski, Anatoli Vasilevich (1875–1933) dramatist (of 14 plays), journalist, critic, literary historian and revolutionary from 1892, becoming a Bolshevik in 1903. After the Bolshevik Revolution, Lenin appointed Lunacharski People's Commissar of Enlightenment (Narkompros) which included all forms of culture. A humanist and pluralist, Lunacharski struggled to preserve the best of Russian culture during and after the Civil War, including churches. He encouraged experimentation as in the work of Mayakovsky, Meyerhold, Mandelshtam and Malevich, and opposed dogmatism and censorship. Appointed Meyerhold director of the Theatre Section. Lunacharski was removed from his post by Stalin in 1929.

Luzhski, Vasili Vasilevich [Kaluzhski] (1869–1931) actor and member of Art Theatre company from its foundation in 1898. A renowned actor whose roles included Sorin in *Seagull*, Professor Serebriakov in *Uncle Vanya*, Andrei Prozorov in *Three Sisters*, understudied Gayev in *Cherry Orchard* and Lebedev in *Ivanov*.

Massalitinov, Nikolai Osipovich (1880–1961) actor, director and pedagogue, he joined the Moscow Art Theatre in 1907, staying until 1919. Became director at the Bulgarian National Theatre in 1925. Played Lopakhin after Leonidov in the MAT's production of *Cherry Orchard*.

Maksimov, Vladimir Vasilevich [Samus] (1880–1937) acted at the Moscow Art Theatre for a single season, 1904–05.

Meiningen/Meininger – see Saxe-Meiningen.

Meshcherskaia, Glama – see Glama.

Meshcherski, Prince Vladimir Petrovich (1839–1914) edited the reactionary weekly *Grazhdanin (Citizen)*, which had considerable influence, its aim being to restore those social conditions which existed prior to the reforms of 1861.

Meyerhold, Vsevolod Emilevich [Meierkhold], [until 1895, Karl Theodor Kasimir] (1874–1940) actor, director, creator of physical movement system called biomechanics. Student of Nemirovich-Danchenko, Moscow's Philharmonic School. Actor with Art Theatre 1898–1902, then 1904–05. Played original Konstantin in 1898 MAT premiere of *Seagull* and other roles. Left to run his own company and Studio affiliated with the MAT. Played first Tuzenbakh in premiere of *Three Sisters*, which Kachalov took over. Acted Trofimov in own production of *Cherry Orchard* three weeks after MAT premiere as Chekhov gave play simultaneously to MAT and Meyerhold. Innovatory productions of Blok, Ibsen, Maeterlinck. Artistic head of Imperial Theatres in St Petersburg, 1908–17. After Revolution, chief of theatrical section of the Commissariat for Enlightenment (Narkompros) under Lunacharski. Experimental productions included Gogol, Mayakovsky, Ostrovski, Chekhov shorts *33 Swoons* (1935). Arrested 1939 and secretly executed under Stalin's purges.

Mikhalkov-Konchalovski, Nikita (1945–) director of the film *Unfinished Piece for Mechanical Piano* (1976) based on Chekhov's *Platonov*. The film is subtitled *Themes from the works of Anton Chekhov*.

Morozov, Savva Timofeevich (1862–1905) businessman and industrialist. Subsidized the formation of the Art Theatre and the construction of the new theatre, becoming a director with Stanislavski and Nemirovich-Danchenko in 1900. After conflict with Stanislavski in support of Gorky, Morozov resigned as a director and withdrew all but minimal financial backing. After the failure of the 1905 Revolution, he committed suicide in Nice.

Moskvin, Ivan Mikhailovich (1874–1946) actor, founder member of the Art Theatre and previously student of Nemirovich-Danchenko's at the Moscow Philharmonic School. Roles in Chekhov's plays included Rode in *Three Sisters* and Yepikhodov in *Cherry Orchard*. Major roles followed as the 'second generation' of MAT actors.

Muratova, Elena Pavlovna (1874–1921) joined the MAT as an actress in 1901, working there until 1921. Parts included Charlotta in the premiere of *Cherry Orchard*.

Nemirovich-Danchenko, Vladimir Ivanovich (1858–1943) dramatist, pedagogue, director, theatre manager and co-founder, with Konstantin Stanislavski, of the Moscow Art Theatre with which he was associated for the rest of his life. It was Nemirovich who championed the work of Chekhov in the 1890's and who returned to him in 1940 with a romantic production of *Three Sisters*.

Nezlobin, Konstantin Nikolaevich [Aliabev] (1857–1930) director, entrepreneur and head of his own Nezlobin Theatre, 1909–17.

Nikolaeva – see Grigoreva.

Ostrovski, Aleksandr Nikolaevich (Alexander Ostrovsky 1823–86) dramatist and regarded as the father of Russian dramatic realism. Ostrovski also initiated important reforms for actors and the theatre. A Russian 19th-century classic, he is still relatively little-known outside Russia. His best-known plays are *Storm (Thunderstorm*, 1860) and *The Poor Bride* (1852) both, like most of his plays, remarkable for the period in sympathy for the position of women. His plays range from comedies to historical dramas, plays about the 'dark' merchant class, and tragedies. After the emancipation of the serfs in 1861, his plays again reflected social changes. His darker plays prompted a famous two-volume essay by the critic N.A. Dobroliubov, *The Dark Kingdom* or *Realm of Darkness*, 1859–62. Most of his plays were staged at the Maly Theatre, to this day called Ostrovski's home.

Pavlov, Polikarp Arsenevich (no dates available) acted at the Moscow Art Theatre, 1908–19.

Petrova, Vera Antonovna (1879–?) a graduate of the Art Theatre school who was a member of the company, 1901–06.

Podgorni, Nikolai Afanasevich (Podgorny, 1879–1947) actor and teacher. Became a member of the Art Theatre in 1903. In 1919 joined the administration of the company. Parts included Fedotik in the premiere of *Three Sisters* and (after Kachalov) Trofimov in *Cherry Orchard*.

Pomialova, Aleksandra Ivanovna [Valts] (1862–?) a ballet dancer who also acted at the Moscow Art Theatre from 1898 to 1905; then again from 1906 to 1909.

Pushkin, Aleksandr Sergeevich (1799–1837) Russia's greatest poet and the virtual founder of modern Russian literature who produced short stories, one-act plays, a novel in verse, *Eugene Onegin* (1823–31); wrote Russia's greatest tragic drama, *Boris Godunov* (1825, published 1831) and, among other works, the tragic *The Queen of Spades* (1833). *Eugene Onegin* and *The Queen of Spades* are also famous from Tchaikovski's operas.

Raevskaia, Evgeniia Mikhailovna [Ierusalimskaia] (1854–1932) acted at Stanislavski's Society of Art and Literature before joining the Moscow Art Theatre at its inception, where she remained for the rest of her life. She also helped organize the theatre's Fourth Studio.

Reinhardt, Max (1873–1943) Austrian director who began his career as an actor before moving to Berlin in 1894, acquiring the Deutsches Theater in 1906 where he staged Ibsen and Wedekind. He also specialized in large-scale, mass productions such as *The Miracle*, staged at the Olympia Stadium in London (1911).

Roksanova, Mariia Liudomirovna [Petrovskaia] (1874–1958) actress and member of the Art Theatre company from 1898. Left in 1902. Parts included Nina in the MAT premiere of *Seagull*.

Rumiantsev, Nikolai Aleksandrovich (1874–1948) acted at the Moscow Art Theatre, 1902–09, and then headed the theatre's financial section until 1925. He emigrated to the United States and ended his days in New York.

Sadovski, Prov Mikhailovich (1874–1947) actor and director who joined the Moscow Maly Theatre in 1895 and spent the remainder of his life there.

Samarova, Mariia Aleksandrovna (1852–1919) acted with the MAT when it opened in 1898. Parts included Marina in the MAT premiere of *Uncle Vanya*.

Sanin, Aleksandr Akimovich [Schoenberg] (1869–1956) directed and acted at the MAT, 1898–1902.

Savitskaia, Margarita Georgevna (1868–1911) a pupil of Nemirovich-Danchenko's at the Moscow Philharmonic School, she was one of the founder members of the Art Theatre where she remained for the rest of her life. With Butova, she was the original Olga in *Three Sisters* (1901).

Saxe-Meiningen, Duke Georg (1826–1914) creator, with his wife Ellen Franz, of a professional theatre company, prompted by director Ludwig Chronegk. Influential company which toured Europe, changing attitudes to realism in staging, historical accuracy, individualized crowd scenes, the emerging roles of director and designer.

Shchepkin, Mikhail Semenovich (1788–1863) serf actor, owned by Count Volkenstein, in 1808 given permission to become a professional actor. Emancipation granted in 1821 after a fund drive to buy his freedom. A long and successful career at the Imperial Moscow Maly Theatre, Shchepkin was called 'the father of Russian realistic acting'. Comic and tragic actor.

Simov, Viktor Andreevich (1858–1935) scenographer and artist. Designed productions at the MAT, 1898–1912 and 1925–35. Among other work, designed all the premieres of Chekhov's plays at the MAT.

Smoktunovski, Innokenti Mikhailovich (1924–94) Russian actor who gained world renown as Hamlet in Kozintsev's film (1964). He joined the Moscow Art Theatre during the 1970s where he played a number of leading Chekhov roles and where he remained until his death.

Snezhin, Boris Mikhailovich [Snigirev] (1875–1936) a graduate of Nemirovich-Danchenko's Moscow Philharmonic School, he acted with the company from 1898 to 1902 and later joined the archival section of the theatre where he worked, more or less continually, for the rest of his life.

Snigirev, Boris Mikhailovich – see Snezhin.

Sosnitski, Ivan Ivanovich (1794–1872) Russian actor who created the role of the mayor in Gogol's *The Government Inspector* (1836).

Stalin, Iosif Vissarionovich [Dzhugashvili] (1879–1953) appointed general secretary of the central committee of the Russian Communist Party in 1922, he remained in that post for the rest of his life. His dictatorial and murderous methods, resulting in the deaths of millions, were condemned by Khrushchev during the 1950s and paved the way for the eventual collapse of the Soviet Union.

Stanislavski, Konstantin Sergeevich [Alekseev] (1863–1938) factory- and land-owner, actor, founder with Nemirovich-Danchenko of Moscow Art Theatre (MKhAT) in 1898. With Nemirovich, directed Chekhov's plays at the Art Theatre. Both directors encouraged such pupils as Meyerhold and Vakhtangov to open Studios affiliated to the MAT. Taught acting to opera singers. Teacher and creator of acting 'system'. Married to actress Lilina.

Stanitsin, Viktor Yakovlevich [Geze] (1897–1976) actor and director at the Moscow Art Theatre Second Studio, 1918–24, when he joined the main company, with which he remained for the rest of his life.

Sumbatov – see Yuzhin.

Suvorin, Aleksei Sergeevich (1834–1912) millionaire St Petersburg newspaper publisher, owner of all railway station newspaper kiosks, editor, theatre critic, and Chekhov's publisher and friend. Suvorin's reactionary political views and his anti-Semitism, particularly over the Dreyfus Affair and conflict over Gorki, damaged their friendship.

Tairov, Aleksandr Yakovlevich [Kornblit] (1885–1950) Soviet director who, together with his actress wife Alisa Koonen, founded their own Kamerny (Chamber) Theatre in Moscow in 1914. Together they staged a range of productions in which aesthetic priorities were paramount in the search for overall artistic unity. Tairov staged a black and white 'concert' production of *Seagull* in 1944.

Tarasova, Alla Konstantinovna (1898–1973) joined the Moscow Art Theatre company in 1916 and acted there for the rest of her life. Her Chekhov roles included Anya in *The Cherry Orchard*, Sonia in *Uncle Vanya*, Irina in *Three Sisters* and Sasha in *Ivanov*.

Tarina, Lidiia Yurevna (no dates available) a graduate of the Moscow Art Theatre School and a member of the company, 1901–05. Played Sasha in MAT premiere of *Ivanov*, 1904, directed by Nemirovich-Danchenko.

Teliakovski, Vladimir Arkadevich (1861–1924) administrative head of Moscow office of the Imperial theatres, 1889–1901; then Director of the Imperial Theatres in both Moscow and St Petersburg, 1901–17. Teliakovski encouraged the Aleksandrinski Theatre's re-staging of *Seagull* in 1902, directed by M.E. Darski, after its disastrous premiere directed by Evtikhi Karpov, 1896.

Tezavrovski, Vladimir Vasilevich (1880–1955) actor, director and a member of the Moscow Art Theatre troupe, 1905–18.

Tikhomirov, Iosaf Aleksandrovich (1872–1908) actor. Student of Nemirovich-Danchenko at Moscow's Philharmonic School. Member of Art Theatre, 1898–1904, as actor and director. Praised for his performance as Medvedenko in the MAT premiere of *Seagull*, 1898.

Tolstoi, Aleksei Konstantinovich (1817–75) dramatist, poet, satirist, novelist. The second part of his dramatic trilogy, *Tsar Fedor/Fiodor* (1868), was the MAT's opening production (Hermitage Theatre, 1898), directed by Stanislavski, designed by Simov.

Tolstoi, Count Lev Nikolaevich (1828–1910) Russian novelist and playwright whose best-known play is his naturalist tragedy of peasant life, *The Power of Darkness* (1886), which was performed at the Moscow Art Theatre in 1902. Among his novels are *War and Peace* and *Anna Karenina*. An admirer of Chekhov's stories, he considered his plays 'as bad as Shakespeare's'. Moralist and philosopher, Tolstoi had many followers.

Tovstonogov, Georgi Aleksandrovich (1915–89) Soviet director of Georgian origin who became artistic director of the Leningrad Bolshoi Drama Theatre in 1957 where he staged a number of outstanding productions, including Chekhov's *Three Sisters* (1965).

Turgenev, Ivan Sergeevich (1818–83) first great novelist of contemporary life. Playwright and 'man of the 40s'. Seminal essay *Hamlet and Don Quixote* (1850). His play *A Month in the Country* (*Mesiats v derevne*, 1849–50) anticipates Chekhov's use of mood and emphasis on character rather than on plot. Directed by Stanislavski at the MAT in 1909.

Vakhtangov, Evgeni Bagrationovich (1883–1922) actor and director who performed minor roles at the Moscow Art Theatre from 1911 to 1912 before helping Stanislavski to found the Art Theatre's First Studio. He went on to stage productions in his own Third Studio (later the Vakhtangov Theatre) concluding with an exhilarating production of Gozzi's *Princess Turandot* (1922) staged in the style of *commedia dell'Arte*. Staged Chekhov's *The Wedding* in 1921, Moscow Art Theatre Third Studio, designed by Isaak Rabinovich. Directed at the MAT First and Third Studios; the Moscow Drama Studio (1914) and the Jewish Habimah Theatre (1918 and 1922).

Varlamov, Konstantin Aleksandrovich (1848–1915) Russian actor who joined the St Petersburg Aleksandrinski Theatre in 1875 and where he remained for the rest of his life, specialising in comic character roles. Chekhov wrote the one-act farce *A Tragic Role* (1889–1890) for Varlamov.

Viazemski, Petr Andreevich (1792–1878) Russian poet and critic who championed the work of Fonvizin, Griboedov and Gogol.

Vishnevski, Aleksandr Leonidovich (1861–1943) actor and founder member of the Moscow Art Theatre. Schoolfriend of Chekhov's. Parts included Dorn in MAT premiere of *Seagull*, the title role in *Uncle Vanya* and Kulygin in *Three Sisters*.

Yefremov, Oleg Nikolaevich (1927–2000) Soviet actor and director, he headed the Sovremennik Theatre in Moscow before being appointed artistic director of the Moscow Art Theatre in 1970 where he staged revitalized productions of all Chekhov's major plays.

Yermolova, Mariia Nikolaevna (1853–1928) a leading actress at Moscow's Maly Theatre, 1871–1921.

Yuzhin, Aleksandr Ivanovich [Sumbatov] (1857–1927) famous actor of Moscow's Maly Theatre, 1882–1927.

Zagarov, Aleksandr Leonidovich [Fessing] (1877–1941) a pupil at Nemirovich-Danchenko's Moscow Philharmonic School who joined the Moscow Art Theatre company in 1898 and stayed there until 1906. Played the stationmaster in the first production of *The Cherry Orchard* (1904), a role introduced in Act III by Stanislavski.

Zhdanova, Mariia Aleksandrovna (1890–1944) acted at the Moscow Art Theatre, 1907–24. Played Anya in the premiere of *Cherry Orchard*.

Zola, Émile (1840–1902) French novelist renowned for exposure of French social reality. 'Creator' of Naturalism. Journalist and polemicist. Imprisoned for his defence of Alfred Dreyfus when he accused the French army and government of anti-Semitism, corruption and cover-up Led the progressives in Europe in Dreyfus's defence and for his release from imprisonment for treason.